THE
SECRET
UNICORN
SOCIETY

T0381973

Published in the UK by Scholastic, 2023
1 London Bridge, London, SE1 9BG
Scholastic Ireland, 89E Lagan Road, Dublin Industrial Estate,
Glasnevin, Dublin, D11 HP5F

Text © Cerrie Burnell, 2023
Cover illustration © Lucy Fleming, 2023
Interior illustrations © Kayt Bochenski, 2023

The right of Cerrie Burnell to be identified as the author of this work has
been asserted by her under the Copyright, Designs and Patents Act 1988.

ISBN 978 0702 32394 2

A CIP catalogue record for this book is available from the British Library.

Printed by CPI Group (UK) Ltd, Croydon, CR0 4YY
Paper made from wood grown in sustainable forests and other controlled sources.

1 3 5 7 9 10 8 6 4 2

www.scholastic.co.uk

THE
SECRET
UNICORN
SOCIETY

CERRIE BURNELL

■SCHOLASTIC

To Darcey and Zac,
keep believing in unicorns.

And to my beautiful Amelie,
keep the magic.

The Unicorn Seekers of South London

A blog by brilliant friends.

Dear Unicorn Seeker

Thanks for stopping by our blog.

Let's begin by telling you the story of how we discovered a unicorn in a South London park at twilight. And not just any unicorn. This was a creature the colour of midnight, with a lightning horn and magnificent wings.

She was extraordinary, magical and heartbreakingly beautiful. Above all, though, she was our friend.

One of the first – and last – of her kind, Astra was being hunted by the Bureau de Secrets (the bad guys). Fortunately, we were able to protect her until she reached her glory (that's what you call a unicorn herd), and her life was saved.

Now she is somewhere on the other side of thunder and we are eating gluten-free croissants and missing her. A lot! So we have sworn allegiance to each other to keep a look out for unicorns and protect them from harm.

These are some of the impossibly possible things we learned along the way, that could help you become a Unicorn Seeker too:

A unicorn can appear at any time – in dreams, at the edge of a lake at dusk or below your bedroom window on a rainy Tuesday evening. Always be ready and never doubt yourself if you see one.

Unicorns move freely among us and stay hidden by appearing to be horses. People who recognize them straight away are official Unicorn Seekers. Being a seeker is a very precious gift, which is sometimes passed down through families but can also just occur naturally. Anyone can see a unicorn if the weather is right. (Hint: look for a mild storm.)

If you want to make friends with a unicorn, always carry a gluten-free muffin, dandelions or thistles, and drop crumbs or petals on the ground. Stand very still at twilight and listen with your heart; you will feel the unicorns' presence more than you will see it.

Remember they are WILD and cannot be tamed. They adore moonlight and respond to LOVE, so always be welcoming and respectful.

All unicorns are different. Some love water, some live for snow, others need sunshine. Use this blog to help you identify the different glories and discover what your unicorn delights in.

If you do lots of seeking and still never see a unicorn - that's OK. Unicorns have to remain a secret. So don't worry at all, just trust that they are there and that they appreciate you thinking of them.

Lastly, if you do find a unicorn and you're worried for its safety, please comment below.

Yours truthfully,

Elodie, Caleb, Marnie-Mae and Kit.

AKA The Unicorn Seekers of South London

CHAPTER ONE

UNICORN DREAMING

In the vast city of London, where the sky can turn from brightest blue to golden grey in the blink of a dreamer's eye, south of the great misty river and opposite a lovely leafy park, lived a girl named Elodie Lightfoot.

Sunlight streamed into the cosy flat where she lived with her dad and her maman, who had recently returned from Paris, making the morning feel almost magical.

Elodie rolled over in bed, yawning herself awake. This had been the first summer in for ever that Elodie's family had spent together. They had strolled round the lake and explored the park with its swooping parakeets and ancient statues like their togetherness was a totally ordinary occurrence.

It wasn't, of course. For years her maman, Esme Lightfoot, had worked away in Paris. Until very recently, Elodie had believed she was working for a fashion house. Then Elodie had learned her maman was actually an undercover agent at the Bureau de Secrets, trying to thwart the Bureau's plans to capture unicorns. Including Astra, the beautiful unicorn Elodie and her friends had found in the park.

Astra…

An image of Astra running through the dark, her horn luminous as she soared towards the moon, galloped through Elodie's mind.

She sat up in bed and pushed the velveteen curtains back, letting the morning flood into her bedroom. Summer was almost over now, and the jewel-green trees by the lake were beginning to turn amber and scarlet. The September sky was bright but cold.

"Six minutes till we leave, Elle. You almost ready?" came her dad's joyful voice from the kitchen.

Elodie blinked her hazelnut eyes, peered at her moon dial clock and rolled out of bed. She wasn't ready at all. In fact, now that Maman was here,

Elodie didn't really need to leave the flat six minutes and one hour after sunrise. She could stay home, take her time, even have a morning bath. But Elodie loved stepping out into the new day with her dad, helping him carry almond butter croissants, oatmeal owls and gluten-free biscuits to the Feather and Fern coffee van so he could sell delicious treats to all of South London. It was all a routine that felt as familiar to Elodie as home itself. Something they had done together for years, and it still felt important.

She twirled around the room, twisting a yellow scrunchie around her masses of curls, being careful not to catch her fingers on the little crackles of lightning that still zipped and glimmered through the ends of her hair. Elodie had once (daringly) used her curls to defuse a net made of lightning, setting Astra free. Although the net was gone, some of the lightning remained like her own little storm. The ponytail turned out slightly wonky, a few curls pinging out at odd angles, but Elodie adored it. No one else had full brown ringlets tinged with the blue gleam of lightning.

Maman's French lullabies carried from the kitchen

along with the scent of Parfum de Rose, and Elodie beamed. If Maman was up and singing, it meant she was coming to the park with them.

Wriggling into her clothes in a giddy dance of joy, she accidentally knocked her thesaurus off her overcrowded bookcase and gave a startled yelp as it almost struck her foot. As she heaved the heavy book back on to its shelf, Elodie caught sight of the little pot of lotion which had belonged to her great-grandmother, Elyse De Lyon, wedged behind a collection of Celtic fairy tales. The pot was the colour of rust and silver and seemed centuries old. It had a mythical winged horse embossed upon its lid.

Not mythical, she thought, her heart aching slightly. *Real.*

Elodie paused as memories of the midnight unicorn, who had appeared in the rain outside her window, rushed once more through her mind.

Astra.

Elodie still missed her so much...

"Elodie!" called Maman. The smell of freshly baked blueberry muffins filled the flat.

"Almost ready!" she yelled, grabbing her school

bag and looping her rainbow-laced roller skates over her shoulders as she rushed into the kitchen to help.

Down the creaky stairs they crept with baskets of fluttery soft croissants, jars of sparkling jam, boxes of banana bread, stacks of vegan biscuits and flasks of organic oat milk.

Elodie tried not to drop anything as they tiptoed past the Singhs' flat on the first floor, hoping not to wake them. Again. But the door flew open and there stood Mrs Singh in her dressing gown and slippers, a tired expression etched across her brow.

"There you are, young Elodie," she said, her gaze softening a little.

"Good morning!" Elodie smiled as she offered her a slice of banana bread. Mrs Singh gladly accepted.

"I've had that dream again. What do you know about the white unicorn?"

Elodie hesitated on the stairs, considering the question as Maman came up behind her.

You see, Elodie wasn't the only one who had the gift. Elle and her maman came from a long line of Unicorn Seekers, but it turned out there were many people from many different families all over the

9

world who had seen unicorns either as children, or in dreams. Only as they'd grown older, they had stopped believing in them and so unicorns had faded into the shadows of their memory.

Mrs Singh was eighty-six years old and her gift had been reawakened when Elodie had smuggled Astra upstairs in the middle of the night to hide her in the bath! Ever since, Mrs Singh's dreams had been filled with unicorns from all different glories, and she took great pride in discussing them with Elodie.

"A white unicorn?" Elodie mused. She'd not heard this unicorn mentioned before.

"Whiter than snow, with a frost-blue mane," continued Mrs Singh. "Ever such noisy hooves ... keeps waking me up. Pirate's very cross about it as I keep disturbing him too."

Pirate was the Singhs' rather grumpy one-eyed cat.

Elodie gave a sympathetic shrug. "I haven't heard anything about a white unicorn, but I'll let you know if I do."

Mrs Singh gave a grateful nod and retreated into her flat.

Elodie's dad was already at the bottom of the stairs leaning on the bright blue front door as it swung open to reveal the sunny September morning.

As Elodie stepped outside, Maman came hurrying behind her with the organic coffee.

"We should pay attention to Mrs Singh's dreams," she said. "The unicorn may be trying to warn her of something."

"But she's always dreaming of unicorns – especially when it rains. Probably just means a storm's coming," Elodie replied, stepping over some late-blooming poppies between the paving stones.

"Perfect weather for croissants," said her dad, grinning as he gestured to the sky.

Elodie and Maman rolled their eyes. "You say that every morning!" they cried, linking arms to cross the empty road and slip almost unseen through the slightly rusted gate and into the lovely leafy park.

It was still peacefully quiet as they made their way around the lake: just the three of them, the ducks and a rare autumn swan. Elodie could not have felt happier.

As her parents busied themselves opening up the

luminous green van, ready for the morning coffee rush, she kicked off her shoes and pulled on her rainbow-laced roller skates, gliding up and down the tree-lined walkway.

Elodie loved this time of morning, when every dream for the day felt possible. The boating lake was smooth as glass, the grass dotted with wildflowers. In the soft early light, if she stared hard enough at the much-loved statues, Elodie could almost imagine them coming to life.

She gazed at the little stag with wonky antlers. He was one of her favourites: slightly smaller than the others, his white paint peeling off with age and the frequent London rain. Sunlight glinted off the water and just for a moment the stag looked brighter, prouder. Did he raise his head? Elodie squinted hard, her heart suddenly dancing with hope. Then clouds rolled across the sky, and the day turned dove-wing grey. The statue was just a statue. Pale and old and lopsided. Elodie let go of the breath she'd been holding.

The sound of wheels whirring over tarmac made her turn and she beamed at Marnie-Mae, her best friend. Marnie-Mae had new hot-pink braids and leopard-print roller skates. She was a self-taught unicorn expert.

"Hiiii," screeched Marnie, zooming over and pulling Elodie into a hug.

"Have a good day, my loves!" called Joni, Marnie-Mae's mum, waving to Elodie's parents as she dashed up the hill towards the train station in extraordinarily high heels.

Joni worked for a make-up company in the city, so Elodie's parents took Marnie-Mae to school and collected her afterwards with Elodie. Both girls loved this arrangement.

"Race you round the lake!" cried Marnie, shooting

off again. As she chased after her, something caught Elodie's eye and she stumbled to a stop, catching her breath. For a fraction of a second, she was certain she'd seen a glowing white horse gallop through the trees. Clearer than moonlight. But all she could see now were bright-winged parakeets, chatting dog-walkers, and people dashing for their morning coffees.

There was no sign of any horse.

Unless...

But Elodie tried not to dwell on that thought.

It must have just been the sunshine, she told herself.

Still, as she skated after Marnie-Mae, Mrs Singh's question rang in her ears: "What do you know about the white unicorn?"

CHAPTER TWO
STRANGE STATUES

Elodie caught up to Marnie-Mae halfway around the lake. Marnie had already forgotten about the race and joined their friend Kit on a park bench instead. Kit and his brother Caleb were home educated – something Elodie envied. They often got to study in the park, which meant they were excellent skaters. Kit preferred roller blades to skates and, with a run up, could jump over a bench in one smooth, soaring motion.

"Hey!" Elodie grinned, flopping down in the middle of the bench. "You guys haven't heard anything about a white unicorn?"

Kit paused for a moment, as if he was trying to remember something, then slowly shook his head.

"Not that I can remember," he said uncertainly.

"Do you know which glory it might be from? A Winter's Dawn? A Twilight Grace?"

"I'm not sure," Elodie replied vaguely. "It's just Mrs Singh keeps having these dreams…"

"There are loads of people who claim they've seen a shiny white unicorn on our blog," sighed Marnie-Mae, rolling her eyes. "I don't believe any of them, but we can go to the computer room and check it out at lunchtime."

The blog had been set up by the four unicorn-seeking friends last summer. It was Marnie's idea and she was super proud of it. To anyone who stumbled across it, it seemed like a perfect work of fiction: gorgeously crafted tales of make-believe unicorn sightings. But really it was a way to connect with other seekers and track the movements of glories all over the globe.

Of course, there were plenty of folk who thought it was all a lovely big pretence. The friends could always tell. But amongst all the tall tales, there were clearly times when sightings were absolutely, dazzlingly real.

Elodie stood up and was about to skate back to

the coffee van when she caught sight of their friend Caleb – Kit's brother. He was standing on the other side of the lake near where the rowing boats were moored and Rufus (his enormous fluffy St Bernard) was flopped lazily at his feet.

Caleb wasn't doing anything in particular except eating a blueberry muffin and carefully sprinkling its crumbs on the ground. Something about the gesture was so tender and familiar it tugged at Elodie's heart. Caleb had been the first member of the Unicorn Seekers' Society before they were even a proper society, their only mission being to find Astra. Elodie knew he missed Astra as much as she did, if not more, and even though it had been months since they'd said goodbye to her, Caleb still scattered crumbs in the park every morning. A tiny act of hope.

Unless … but no … there couldn't be. Was it possible Caleb had seen another unicorn and the others were yet to find out about it?

Elodie wrestled with her thoughts. She could ask Caleb of course. He was usually very keen to talk about the things he loved, but he seemed deep in thought and she didn't want to startle him by calling out across the lake.

And he looked so chilly this morning, snuggled up in a chunky woollen scarf, every colour of the rainbow. As if he was fending off the cold. It felt too warm to Elodie for such a huge scarf. But Caleb didn't always wear clothes that were in harmony with the weather. He wore clothes that brought him joy, comfort and happiness.

Elodie turned to Kit. "Your brother hasn't mentioned anything about any other unicorns, has he?"

"Not to me," Kit replied.

"Elle, Marnie, time for school!" came Maman's voice from the Feather and Fern.

"We've got to go," Elodie said, grasping Marnie's hand and skating back around the lake to grab their stuff.

The image of the glowing white horse stayed with Elodie all day, like the haunting memory of a dream you've half forgotten. Every time she pictured it, her heart raced and her curls quietly crackled.

Thankfully, the school day rushed by in a blur of learning and laughter. Marnie-Mae found nothing particularly enlightening about a mysterious white unicorn on the blog at lunchtime – only some super fans from Paris, who believed there was a unicorn living on their balcony. They didn't give a description, so Marnie didn't buy it. Then there was a woman from California, who claimed she'd had a pet unicorn the colour of stardust for years – along with two white tigers. Marnie could definitely believe this, but if the unicorn wasn't in danger, then she could take her time and reply another day. A grandmother from Germany believed she'd seen an entire glory of magnificent midnight unicorns fly over the top of a house. Her description was impeccable.

"Sounds accurate!" Marnie beamed.

When the final bell of the day rang, Marnie had to get to drama club, while Elodie went to the art room. She was working on a design for the *Unicorn Seekers Society* official badge. So far, she'd made a graceful unicorn head in profile from black sequins, with moon-bright eyes and a glittery gold horn. It was going to take a little while to finish, but Elodie was sure it would be worth the time.

Once she'd mastered one, she could easily make three more. Then they could all sew them on to their jackets.

Somehow, this little act of joy made her feel closer to Astra.

As she stitched a line of sequins in place, a boy she hardly knew came into the busy art room. He was a year older than her and she didn't even know his name.

"Hi ... I'm Rishi," he said a little nervously, looking only at Elodie.

Elodie looked up in surprise.

"Oh! Hi, I'm Elodie," she replied kindly over the hum of sewing machines.

Rishi shifted his weight from foot to foot, staring at the ground, before clearing his throat.

"Do you like ... run that blog thing about imaginary beasts?"

Elodie sat up a little straighter. She knew loads of people thought the blog was a joke, that there couldn't possibly have been a unicorn being hunted across South London.

But Elodie, Marnie, Kit and Caleb knew better.

"My friend Marnie-Mae runs the Unicorn Seekers blog. I'm one of the seekers," she said with a quietly proud smile.

"So, like, you think it's all real then?" Rishi mumbled, looking very uncomfortable and crumpling something in his hands.

"Unicorns are real," said Elodie firmly. "The blog is for people who are seekers or hope to become part of our society."

The rest of the people in the art room were beginning to stare and softly giggle.

Rishi gave a quick nod.

"Cool. Cool, just checking," he said, dropping something on the floor, before turning and leaving the room.

Elodie gave a long sigh as the other kids mumbled and whispered around her. She ignored them and turned her attention back to her sewing.

Later, as the afternoon sun warmed the waters of the lake, Marnie hugged Elodie goodbye and skated off into her mum's arms. Elodie laughed and waved goodbye. It was a relief to not feel any of the sharpness of missing Maman, a feeling she'd struggled with for years when Maman had been away. Though Elodie understood the importance of Maman's work as a double agent for the Ministry of Magical Creatures – a network of gifted seekers who guarded the *Map of Lost Unicorns* book and protected the glories – it hadn't stopped her missing her.

She skated off to find her beloved maman, who she knew would be chatting to the regulars at the Feather and Fern to see what they thought of the new apricot croissants.

She took the longer route as the evening was still light and full of September's first falling leaves.

As she raced over the gravel track, Elodie took in all of the familiar scenery. That was the beautiful thing about the park: it was bejewelled with history, nature and a bright feeling of timeless wonder. She particularly loved the site where the Palace of Crystal had once stood. This palace had long ago been home to Princess Grace, who shared the gift for seeing unicorns. Princess Grace had sketched many of them in this very park. And it was through her artistry that Elodie and her friends had learned about the different glories – herds of unicorns.

She darted past the maze and old stage, then flew down the main tree-lined walkway towards the Feather and Fern. Leaning in to the breeze, she gazed at the oddly shaped dinosaurs hidden amongst the trees. They were huge. Some of them comical, others vividly regal, and they gave the park a surreal feeling of enchantment.

Her eyes came to rest on the slightly lopsided little white stag. He was sweet and always made Elodie chuckle. His paint may be peeling off but his eyes still seemed to be smiling.

Her hair had begun to crackle fiercely. As she stared at it, the statue seemed to glow brighter, and suddenly Elodie was sure that she could hear the patter of hooves, light as thistledown. She stumbled, hit a small rock and tumbled on to the dusty ground. She shot back up instantly, ignoring her scraped knees.

Her heart was still skipping, her hair fizzing with little bolts of lightning. But the statue was simply a statue. Yet that feeling, that pull of certainty that something wonderful was about to unfold, would not cease.

Elodie stood quite still, staring at the stag, willing him to move and hoping the lightning storm in her hair would settle. Eventually, she tore herself away and in a flurry of determination, she slipped out of the park's rusted gate, carefully crossed the road, opened the bright blue door and clattered up the stairs, still in her roller skates.

Bursting into her bedroom, Elodie freed her hair from its scrunchie, so the little storm erupting in her curls could defuse, then grabbed the ancient, rusted pot and sat down on her bed. It looked like a tub of specialist hair lotion. For years Elodie had believed that was all it was. But now she knew the truth. This was no ordinary lotion. It had been gifted to her great-grandmother Elyse de Lyon by a unicorn, under circumstances that were too sad for Elodie to think about. Just a dab of the lotion would help Elodie know if there was a unicorn out there.

The lid slid open, and at once the entire room filled with the aroma of rain on a midsummer's eve.

Then came the rushing saltiness of the sea, followed by the swift and heartbreaking sense of melting snow. And just for a moment, there was a final sensation, one which Elodie now knew to be the smell of moonlight.

Closing her eyes, she let the scent wash over her. She felt touched by a warm golden glow as the sounds of the world outside of her window hushed, and the only thing she could hear was the rhythm of her heart. Slow and steady, like the pounding hooves of a horse: swift, wild and graceful. And just for a moment she saw it. Or did she feel it?

A unicorn the colour of a winter moon, charging in anger, its mane blue with rage, and beside it a little shadow.

Dear Seekers,

I'm crossing my fingers and toes that this reaches you in time. I felt too shy to write to you on the blog, in case my friends found out. I really hope you understand. You see, I think a unicorn is in serious danger.

Like, a real unicorn, not a made-up one. An actual mythical creature with a horn that only appears in the twilight rain.

This is how I found him.

Three nights ago, I discovered a horse in our community garden, hiding under the apple trees behind the recycling bins.

He was snow-white and very majestic. He looked like a regular horse, only his mane was blue, like ice in the moonlight.

I showed him to all of my friends who live in my block, and they thought he was pretty cool. We fed him apples, took selfies with him and even named him Nigel.

But then there was a storm - do you remember? On Saturday. Not a really bad storm, but rainy enough that everyone ran inside when it started. I stayed with Nigel. I wanted to make sure he was OK and I kind of felt responsible for him. I didn't know if I should get my mum to call a vet or something.

But I was amazed to find that Nigel loved the rain! And he wasn't afraid of thunder one bit. He kept chasing the clouds across the garden, trampling the vegetable patch with his huge hooves. That's when I realized his hooves weren't really like an ordinary horse's at all. They looked like they were made from crystal or glass. . .

Then, suddenly, lightning struck and it was like time stopped. Like the world fell away and it was just me and Nigel and he was the king of storms and all the lightning poured down from the sky, straight into him.

Then I saw the horn. It just appeared in the storm. And I realized Nigel definitely wasn't a lost "horse"; he was something completely mythical. The horn looked like sea-glass. Like a dream made real. Right here in the Oak Grove community garden. I've never known anything like it. I would have stayed with him for ever, but at some point, my mum started calling to me from the balcony, shouting that I had to come in for my tea.

I gave Nigel some extra apples and was wondering if I should get him a blanket, when he looked at me very directly and I sort of felt that Nigel really wasn't the right name for him. At all. I felt that his true name was. . .

Jordash.

I know it sounds silly, but I started calling him Dash right away. It just felt right. I never planned to become a unicorn seeker – it just happened, and that's why I'm super relieved I found you.

You see, I think Dash is in some kind of trouble. Once all my family had gone to bed, I snuck out on to the balcony to check on him. He was standing – gleaming – behind the recycling bins, brighter than a full moon and so striking. The night was cool, but without any warning it became icy cold, as if the air had changed.

Dash leapt right over the bins, reaching an astonishing height, and charged away into the night. I wanted so badly to go after him, but moments later a huge van pulled up right outside the gardens and three very serious looking men got out.

Their voices were low and they were speaking in a language I didn't understand. They were acting strangely and searching around, wrecking the vegetable patch even more. Then I realized: they were looking for Dash . . . and now I'm really worried.

I know this may sound silly, but it's all totally true. Something was in the van and it was thrashing and bashing around so much that one of the men opened the side door just a little way to throw in some apples (that they stole from our garden).

I only caught a glimpse, but whatever was inside was pure, brilliant white. Whiter than bone, with an icy blue aura. I swear it was another unicorn, like Dash but smaller. She looked like she was in some sort of electric cage . . . a cage made from lightning?

I don't know. Anyway – I think those men might have been trying to capture Dash. He escaped this time, but I'm worried they might try again.

Perhaps they're zookeepers and they're trying to rescue him. But somehow I don't think so. . .

If this makes any sense to you, please write back.

Your new friend Rishi

Sycamore class

CHAPTER THREE

MIDNIGHT MOONLIGHT

Something woke Elodie and she sat up in bed, her hair a cluster of luminous sparks. She felt both too hot and briskly cold at the same time.

She had fallen asleep with the velveteen curtains wide open and the jar of lotion from her great-grandmother Elyse clasped firmly in her hand. Silvery, soft moonlight flooded the room, shining directly on to Elodie's pillow.

The moon must have woken me...

She glanced at the moon dial clock and her eyes opened wide in anticipation as she read the time: seven minutes past midnight. The exact time that she'd first seen Astra.

Elodie gave a hard shudder as she became aware

33

of how freezing cold it was for a September night, and she wriggled quickly into her polka-dot dressing gown. Peering at the empty street below, she studied the lamplight and leafy shadows, hoping against hope that a unicorn had run through her dreams to wake her.

A tiny crystalline snowflake twirled on the breeze, glittering whimsically before it danced away.

The tick of the moon dial clock grew louder and Elodie froze, holding her breath.

Faintly, as if from a great distance, Elodie heard a rhythm. It reminded her of wild winter wind and icy tides. Something began to sparkle at the edge of Elodie's mind, as if it were rushing through the city to reach her.

She gasped, trying to contain her excitement as the thrum of powerful hooves came closer and a moon-kissed horse, as bright as silver lightning, broke from the treeline, leaping over the park fence and hurtling along the pavement.

This time Elodie knew instantly that the fearless horse was a unicorn. This time she didn't hesitate.

As the unicorn sped towards her, Elodie raced out

of the little flat, crossing the landing and running flat-out down the stairs. She reached the front door and pulled it open. A frozen whirl of icy wind brushed lightly on her cheeks.

The unicorn was charging straight down the road. It was huge! Easily as big as a shire horse, its gleaming, near-translucent hooves seemed to spin the air into stardust. Its thick blue mane shimmered in the wind and its eyes were so icy it was like gazing at the surface of a frozen lake.

One glance and Elodie felt a deep affinity for this astonishing creature. She stepped breathlessly into the street. Clouds whipped across the sky and the night darkened to a deep velvet. Little snowflakes drifted above and in the glow of the lamplight Elodie saw the dagger-sharp gleam of the unicorn's horn.

It was all the colours of ice beneath the aurora, and as lovely as twilight on a winter's eve.

A Winter's Dawn, Elodie breathed, knowing at once that this was the unicorn's glory.

As its blazing blue eyes locked with hers, a name flickered through her mind, fast as a shooting star that she couldn't quite grasp.

Elodie opened her arms, reaching out in welcome, not minding the soft snow on her skin. But the unicorn did not slow down. It fled past her, and she lost the threads of its name and felt instead only a rushing, thundering panic.

Elodie spun in bewilderment, wondering if she should run after the unicorn, when all at once, she felt Maman's firm hands on her shoulders pulling her swiftly back into the hallway and quickly closing the bright blue door.

"Come away, *ma petite fille*, it's not safe," she whispered, putting a finger to her lips as another door opened further up the stairs and light spilled out.

"I knew that noisy unicorn was in trouble," clucked Mrs Singh, as she fastened her dressing gown. "Come in, come in and I'll show you."

Before they knew it, Elodie, Maman and Mrs Singh – plus a rather furious Pirate the cat – were crouched in the living room of the Singhs' flat, looking in rigid silence through the cracks of the shuttered blind.

At first, all they could see was wild weather and an alarmed fox. But moments later a large grey van rattled down the road at break-neck speed. A faint melody of music coming from within. A fearsome whinny split the silence and Elodie heard the manic pounding of hooves. Still, there was no unicorn in sight.

As the van passed below, Elodie, Maman and Mrs Singh all drew back, gasping as a deep feeling of unease settled in Elodie's stomach.

Elodie's hair danced around in a high halo of

lightning, her heart desperately aching.

Something was very wrong.

"What was in the van?" she asked, staring at Maman, who was standing stone still.

"I believe it's a unicorn," answered Mrs Singh, settling into her favourite chair, sipping a very large cup of sweet milky tea.

"But how? And who on earth was driving that van?"

Maman shook her head. "Not anyone I've ever seen, but there are many people who hunt unicorns, not to mention the Bureau de Secrets. I can ask my network to see what they know."

Elodie nodded. She was still very shaken.

"But you need three things to catch a unicorn, don't you?" she whispered.

Maman nodded. *"The Map of Lost Unicorns,* a Unicorn Seeker with the gift of unicorn sight and a net made of lightning."

"They don't have the book," Elodie murmured, "but they must have a lightning net, and one of those men must be a seeker."

Maman gave a long sigh. "A very gifted seeker,

I should imagine. They've already captured one unicorn and are using it as bait to draw the wild unicorn out."

"So not everyone needs the book?" Mrs Singh frowned.

Maman gave a tired shrug.

"The book tells you everything you could ever hope to know about unicorns, including how to catch them. But it's possible to do your own studying. If you only wanted to capture a specific unicorn, the *Map of Lost Unicorns* might not be necessary."

Elodie gave an angry groan and opened the shutters, pushing at the window and leaning out in the night. She took a deep breath and let the cool air soothe her soul and calm her hair.

The unicorn and the van were gone. The street was quiet and empty but for the swimming reflection of stars upon the puddles.

"We should follow the van and make them stop so we can free the captured unicorn," Elodie pleaded.

"We will do no such thing," said Maman indignantly and Pirate purred in agreement.

But Elodie's heart lurched. Maman couldn't

expect her to do nothing. She couldn't possibly just wait for someone else to help the trapped unicorn. It went against the unicorn seeker's code. Yet as she stared sadly at the grown-ups in the room, she saw it had already been decided.

Maman would investigate things tomorrow, the official way.

But Elodie could not bear to wait. Not while a unicorn was in danger…

Once they'd said goodnight to Mrs Singh and tiptoed back to their own little flat, Elodie lay in her bed refusing to sleep. She would make her own plan. She just needed to wait until Maman was sound asleep.

Yet her room felt so snug and cosy after the sharpness of the icy wind, and Elodie's eyelids felt so heavy, like they were laden with snow.

Sitting up abruptly, Elodie shook herself awake and yanked her school bag out from under her bed. She couldn't risk falling asleep. She could at least try and do some homework to keep her mind busy.

As she opened the bag, a badly crumpled note fell out on to her duvet. Carefully, Elodie opened it up and turned on her reading torch. Her mouth fell open as she read the note in stunned silence, the glimmer of the frost unicorn's name hovering at the edge of her thoughts, just out of reach.

Jordash…

Or Dash, she thought brightly.

As the moon dial clock struck 1 a.m., Elodie scurried into the kitchen, seized her dad's phone and sent a message:

Unicorn sighting at seven minutes past midnight. Emergency Unicorn Seekers meeting tomorrow at the lake before school.

She climbed back into bed and was asleep in minutes, tiny flecks of lightning still glittering in her curls.

CHAPTER FOUR
SNOW IN THE PARK

The next morning at six minutes past sunrise, Elodie was up racing around the kitchen, turning on the oven, preparing the gluten-free croissants and ensuring her dad made an extra batch of blueberry muffins. She was desperate to get to the park for the morning meeting.

The dawn beyond her window was a clear, crisp pink, gently brightening to blue, and she could hear the birds singing. But the memory of the white unicorn and the strange van weighed on Elodie's mind.

Maman was sleeping in late, her silken sleep mask shielding her eyes, and for the first time that Elodie could remember, she and her dad left the flat early!

It was quite a lovely feeling.

The morning felt serenely calm and after helping set up the Feather and Fern, Elodie soared off around the lake on her roller skates, her restless energy driving her forward in long smooth glides. As she skated, she began to gather her thoughts to share with the Unicorn Seekers. Autumn sunshine warmed her face as the park came to life.

She paused where the rowing boats were moored, gazing out at the swans and black-necked geese. A sharp little breeze whipped through her hair, making her shiver. Elodie drew her cardigan tightly around her, rolling backwards into the shade beneath a canopy of scarlet-leafed trees. At once the air turned icy and she noticed a spider's web strung between two branches, draped in droplets of dew that had frozen solid like a beautiful winter ornament.

As she reached out to gently touch it, the memory of the white unicorn charging down her street came to her: how the night had turned to winter, and the air had been full of tiny specks of snow.

She turned abruptly on her stopper, peering into the dense thicket of woodland behind her. This was the exact spot where Caleb had been stood yesterday, lovingly sprinkling muffin crumbs.

At once, Elodie's gaze flew to the ground, searching for the little crumbs. But they were gone. She supposed this wasn't strange for a busy city park. Any number of woodland animals could have gobbled them up, from green-winged parakeets to water rats or squirrels.

Then something fluttered towards her, soft as a feather, bright as a star. Elodie gasped in delight as it settled coldly on her nose.

A snowflake! Just like last night...

Elodie closed her eyes, standing completely still as she leaned into the feeling of winter, letting her heart pick up the rhythm of the woods and trying to sense the rush and canter of frosted hooves. But she felt only stillness, as if the woods were keeping their secrets.

She sighed and skated away. Either the little cocoon of winter chill was just weird London weather, or...

This is where the winter unicorn is hiding, and it really doesn't want to be found.

Either way, she needed to speak to her friends. Especially Caleb.

Twenty minutes later, the Unicorn Seekers' Society (and a dozing Rufus) were huddled beneath a large oak tree on the other side of the park, near the skate ramps. Trying not to mumble too inconspicuously, or shout too loudly, they read the letter from Rishi together.

"So we know there are two unicorns," Kit said, taking notes. His notebook was his favourite thing. He had bought it especially for recording unicorn discoveries and was very proud of how official – yet boring – it looked. Like it could have simply been a book of accounts, or shopping lists. Something no one would pay attention to.

But if you dared to peek between the covers, you would find a glorious study of unicorns.

"I bet the frost unicorn you saw last night is the same one that Rishi found in the Oak Grove community garden," said Kit excitedly.

"And probably the same one that keeps waking Mrs Singh," added Marnie, who sounded wildly excited to finally be on the trail of an actual unicorn. Not just a sighting someone had dreamed up on the blog.

"I think both unicorns – the captured one and the wild one, Dash – are from the same glory, a Winter's Dawn," added Elodie.

"Or even the same family," said Caleb under his breath.

"What's your mum saying about it?" asked Marnie-Mae.

"She doesn't know who the people in the van are, but she's going to speak with her network," Elodie explained.

Everyone nodded – they knew that Elodie's mum belonged to the Ministry of Magical Creatures.

"So we need to find Dash before those guys in the van do," declared Kit.

"I think one of them must be a seeker gone bad, so we need to be quick," added Elodie. "I'll speak to Rishi and see if Dash has gone back to the community garden," she offered.

"I'll check our copy of the Map of Lost Unicorns to see if there's anything we've missed about Winter's Dawns," said Kit.

"I'll keep an eye on the blog," offered Marnie.

"Caleb, can you do some research and see if there's

any other folklore online?" asked Kit.

"Sure," Caleb replied. "Or I could just tell you everything I've learned about them instead. It would be much quicker."

The group went quiet for a moment.

"Caleb, have you seen the wild unicorn in the park?" asked Elodie gently.

Caleb nodded.

"So you've seen Dash?" asked Marnie, who was clearly fighting the urge to leap to her feet and race off to find Dash right this very minute.

Caleb shook his head. "Not just Dash."

"Both of the white unicorns?"

"Not the unicorn in the van," said Caleb.

Everyone looked slightly bewildered. Elodie turned to him.

"Caleb, when you said they might be a family … what did you mean?"

"I'll show you, but you have to PROMISE to keep it a secret."

Kit laid a gentle hand on his brother's arm.

"We won't tell anyone, Caleb. Not Mum, or Sammy next door, or anyone on the blogs."

Caleb looked uncertain.

"And we won't take any pics," piped up Marnie. Secretly, she wondered how on earth she would manage to keep this promise but knew deep down that she would never risk the safety of a unicorn, nor Caleb's friendship.

"We don't even have to add it to the Map of Lost Unicorns," said Elodie, her voice warm with understanding. She knew the depth of responsibility and the sleepless whispering worry of protecting unicorns. Especially if they were in real danger.

"OK. But wrap up warm," said Caleb, shooting off over the gravelly path in a cloud of dust. The others tailed him on roller skates, like a colourful procession.

Caleb skated in a ring around the park, coming to an easy halt beneath the canopy of scarlet-leafed trees, near where the rowing boats were moored.

Kit, Marnie and Elodie came to a halt a little way behind him. They clasped each other's hands and stared at Caleb in anticipation.

A strange silence descended, making everyone shiver.

"What's going on?" Marnie-Mae mouthed, as a

snowflake settled on one of her hot-pink braids.

"We have to wait for her to come to us," said Caleb crossly, wishing the others would remember to be patient *and* quiet.

And so they stood in silence, pretending to be patient.

Again, Elodie closed her eyes, letting the cold wash over her like a soft familiar magic. Seeing if she could hear the same soft rhythm of the previous night.

At first, she felt nothing.

Then, there came the tiniest, gentlest patter of hooves. It was nothing like the wild galloping rush of Dash's hooves, but it stirred her heart with hope.

All at once the day seemed brighter, the air full of frost. Beside her, Marnie-Mae and Kit both gasped in awe and as Elodie opened her eyes, she saw why.

Before them was a foal, no bigger than a newborn. Its coat was purest white with patches of pink, its hooves could have been carved from ice, and its eyes were the wintry blue of sapphires.

But it was the little creature's horn that stole her breath. Transparent as rain, yet beautifully luminous, as if it could cut through the fabric of the world.

Just like Astra's.

CHAPTER FIVE

THE FERAL FOAL

Elodie, Kit and Marnie-Mae froze as a million myths became real for them once more.

Even though they had all seen a unicorn before. Even though they had spent the summer dashing around Europe to save one. Even though they had all been dazzled by the gleam and glare of Astra's horn ... None of them had ever seen a foal. The surreal, heart-soaring wonder of discovering such a young unicorn near the boating lake on a Tuesday morning was so otherworldly, it felt as though they'd stumbled into a dream.

"OMG it's adorable," Marnie-Mae whispered, clasping her hands firmly together so she wouldn't break her promise by taking a photo.

"It's so weirdly sweet… What do we call it?" murmured Kit, staring in amazement at the wild little thing, which kept trotting on the spot, then jumping up randomly as if she were a kitten.

Elodie was silenced by the sheer magnificence of their discovery. It was one of the loveliest things she'd ever seen.

"She doesn't have a name yet really," Caleb explained in a low tone. "But I call her Stormy."

The name was perfect, but at its mention, Rufus gave a low growl – or was it a whimper? – and slunk behind Caleb's legs.

Caleb ruffled Rufus's fur, then moved lovingly towards the little creature, offering her a nibble of muffin. Elodie noticed he was careful to sprinkle it on the ground.

She wondered if Stormy was too shy to be fed from his hand.

The little unicorn skipped proudly forward, gobbling up the muffin and shaking out her blue mane. The dazzle of snow and sun reflecting off her horn was like a wintry rainbow. Then she looked up, her ears pricked and her sapphire eyes twinkling.

"Everyone move," ordered Caleb rather urgently, turning on his roller blades and pushing Rufus out of the way.

"Why?" Marnie-Mae tried to ask, but Caleb grabbed her wrist and pulled her aside. In seconds, Stormy had changed completely. She charged towards them, her horn down like a little raging bull. Caleb and Marnie stumbled backwards into some heather, trying not to panic.

The baby unicorn danced in a circle, then headed straight for Elodie and Kit. They both dived out of the way, landing softly on a crisp pile of leaves.

The creature whinnied fiercely and bounded over the two friends, as agile as a mountain goat.

A furious flurry of snowflakes descended and Stormy leapt lightly up into the boughs of a large cherry tree. But the branches of the tree weren't wide enough, and her hooves clattered and scattered as she tried to clamber skyward.

For a moment she paused, seeming to have found harmony with the wind and the tree. Elodie gave a gasp of relief.

"Watch out!" yelled Kit, as the branch supporting

Stormy wobbled, bent and then snapped clean away. With a bray of unbridled joy, the little unicorn tumbled to the ground, landing dangerously close to Marnie, Caleb and Rufus.

"She's out of control!" yelped Marnie, pushing herself out of the heather as Rufus burrowed deeper in order to hide. Stormy struck her crystalline hoof against the ground and swished her fabulous mane as if she were preparing to fight a lion.

Marnie screamed, trying to duck, but the gleaming point of Stormy's dagger-sharp horn cut straight through one of her braids.

"How do we calm her down?" hissed Kit, but Caleb only shrugged. "We just have to wait. She's only a baby."

"That could take for ever and we've got to get back to Mum soon."

"Well, we can't just abandon a feral baby in the park," chimed in Elodie, a little nervously. "What if someone sees her? She's so excitable. Someone's bound to notice. Caleb, how do you manage to keep her hidden?"

"I don't do anything. She hides herself, in the lake."

Kit, Marnie and Elodie all stared at him in astonishment.

"You mean she leaps in here?" cried Marnie, pointing at the lake.

Caleb winced in horror, covering his eyes with his hands, knowing exactly what would happen next. Stormy suddenly bucked, then cantered straight towards the little fence that ran around the edge of the lake. In one fabulously smooth bound, she cleared it, crashed over a few rowing boats and splashed into the water, terrifying two coots and alarming a swan.

Elodie had never scrambled to her feet so quickly in all her life. She hardly knew if she was skating or falling, but she reached the little fence breathless, Kit and Marnie-Mae behind her.

"Where'd she go?" Marnie asked.

They searched the surface of the lake for a glimpse of their fierce little friend, but there was nothing to be seen. She had vanished like a mermaid diving to the depths of the sea. Before long, the lake was serenely calm once again.

"I don't understand," said Kit, brushing some of the dust off his knees. Despite the spell of snow, he was feeling quite hot and bothered and a bit annoyed that Caleb had found the unicorn first.

"None of the entries in the Map of Lost Unicorns mention anything about Winter's Dawns residing underwater. Apart from the manuscript from Byron Bjornson. The arctic explorer, remember? He mentions unicorns being smart about concealing themselves and swimming beneath the sea. We need to find out more. Surely she can't stay in there all day?"

"Let's ask Caleb," said Elodie, turning to see him

sitting beneath a large oak tree, soothing a rather vexed Rufus. She noticed that Caleb didn't seem so worried himself.

"She hides out in the lake all the time," he explained, wishing the others wouldn't crowd him. "It's her safe place. She can stay in there until twilight and no one ever seems to see her."

"That's lucky," said Marnie, who couldn't help but love the little beast, even if she had lost a braid to her.

"Not all unicorns can stay underwater," said Elodie, sadly remembering the tale of the gallant unicorn who had given its life to save her great-grandmother when she'd fallen into a lake.

A sharp whistle interrupted them from across the park.

"That's my dad!" Elodie exclaimed. "I don't want to leave Stormy, but we can't be late for school." Her heart ached with worry but she felt reassured by Caleb's calm.

"We'll research Winter's Dawns … and sea horses! And find out what we can," Kit said encouragingly as they all dusted the gravel from the backs of their legs.

"We'll track down Rishi and see if we can find out more about Dash." Marnie beamed.

"I just can't believe we found a baby unicorn. Do you think she's Dash's foal?" said Elodie dreamily.

"She is," answered Caleb. "I've seen them together."

Elodie's eyes opened very wide.

"So the other unicorn in the van must be…"

"Stormy's mum."

Marnie-Mae put her hands over her mouth.

"So those awful van men have separated a mother from its baby and are now using her as bait to capture the whole family!" she said hotly.

"Well, that's a bad move. My mum said you should never get between a mother and her baby, it's really dangerous," added Kit.

Elodie reached out a hand to Marnie-Mae. Marnie-Mae smiled and took one of Kit's hands in hers, while Kit and Elodie gently each laid a hand upon Caleb's shoulders. Beneath the canopy of leaves they recited the Unicorn Seekers' oath.

"From sunrise to midnight,
Through sunshine and snow,
We'll protect unicorns

Wherever we go."

"Let's meet by the ice-cream van after school," called Marnie as the four friends skated off in opposite directions.

It wasn't until lunchtime that Elodie and Marnie-Mae found their way to Sycamore class. Rishi was perched on a school bench just outside, playing a game of Lucky Sevens. As soon as he locked eyes with Elodie, he dropped his fan of cards, muttered an apology to his friends, and approached the two girls shyly.

"I got your letter," said Elodie brightly.

"Oh yeah, right," Rishi began. "You think I'm one of those weird people on the blog, don't you?"

"We believe you," cut in Marnie-Mae. "We've seen your unicorn too, or at least Elle has … and her mum … and her eighty-six-year-old neighbour."

"Right … makes sense," said Rishi, looking as if none of it made any sense at all.

"It's a lot to take in," Elodie explained gently, "but you're a true Unicorn Seeker, one of the real ones, with the gift. Not everyone can actually see unicorns, even though they've always existed among us. Most people just see them as horses and don't give them a second glance."

Rishi nodded, still looking a little bewildered, but there was a twinkle beginning to form in his eyes.

"We need you to show us where you last saw Dash," said Marnie-Mae in a dramatic whisper.

"We know he's in a lot of danger," Elodie explained, "but if we can find him, we can help him."

"I saw him this morning when I gave him some breakfast. He's still hiding out behind the recycling bins at Oak Grove community garden."

"What are you doing after school today?" asked Elodie in a rush of wild hope. "We really need to find that unicorn. But first we'll introduce you to the rest of the Unicorn Seekers' Society."

Taken from the diary of Ava Bjornson,
sister of the late explorer Byron Bjornson.

November 30th 1916
Day one, twilight

Oh, how it fills my heart to be continuing my late brother's legacy. And in secret!

The journey here was long, dark and exceptionally cold, even for a Nordic lass like me. For after I fled from the church, escaping a life I didn't choose, I had only a lacy wedding dress, a stolen fur coat and slippers. These were no match for the frozen north.

But I knew I could do it. I knew I was right to come.

I arrived this morning to a dark and stormy sea, full of reflected stars. As expected, there is only an hour of sunlight here each day. Thankfully, a herd of mysterious white horses helped to push my raft ashore and a beautiful young woman from the fishing village found me a spare woollen shawl and some winter boots.

I soon realized that the white horses that saved me were not horses at all. They were creatures of folklore. The very creatures my brother had been tracking.

After consulting my late brother's notes, I can confidently confirm those creatures were unicorns, born of snow and starlight. The unicorns are luminous and inspire delight. They are drawn to storms and lightning and they have a particular love of the sea. I've now observed them surviving many hours underwater in freezing conditions.

I have named this herd Winter's Dawn, and I believe that the sea is their safety, for they can remain hidden beneath the crashing waves. I don't know if they can breathe underwater, or just hold their breath for long stretches of time, but I am hoping to find out.

These creatures are so fiercely intelligent, though those glassy horns look deathly sharp to me.

I share my brother's awe. I too feel as if I have never witnessed anything so extraordinary. I was right to escape my awful engagement. I have no regrets about running away from that boring man at the church, selling my diamond engagement ring to fund my trip, and boarding a ship.

I will never return! I will instead stay and nurture the

unicorns, studying them and helping them in any way I can. In many ways, this helps me feel closer to my brother.

Perhaps I will fall in love with the woman from the fishing village and make a home with her here. Or perhaps I will become an intrepid explorer, like my brother always believed I could be.

I cannot wait for day two of my new life. A life of magic, wonder and dreams made real.

CHAPTER SIX

MOONFLOWERS

At four o'clock on Tuesday afternoon, Rishi, the entire Unicorn Seekers' Society and Rufus were stood on the edge of Oak Grove community garden, beneath the shade of a sweetly scented, golden-brown pear tree.

Marnie-Mae had had the brilliant idea to email Kit and Caleb from the school computer to inform them of the change in location for that afternoon's meeting. The two brothers had eagerly persuaded their mum, Sophia, to let them come and she'd cycled over with them as they skated in front. Neither Sophia nor Rishi's mum minded at all that their children were taking an interest in an award-winning community garden and were more than happy to sit beneath the pear tree, sipping cups of fresh mint tea from their flasks as they exchanged tips on meditation practices. "OK, the grown-ups are distracted," whispered Kit, as the five children and the big shaggy dog made their way as casually as possible towards the recycling bins.

"Here." Rishi indicated, pointing to a little dark alleyway just behind the bins.

And there, shining like a northern star on the darkest night, was a unicorn the brilliant white of snow beneath moonlight. He was curled up like an enormous white dragon, his horn invisible and his eyes firmly closed.

Rufus gave a low woof of surprise and the unicorn's bright blue eyes snapped open. Slowly he raised his regal head and shook his icicle-blue mane.

Elodie shivered, feeling the air turn colder, but the sight of the mysterious unicorn soothed her.

"He's pretty docile in the daytime," Rishi whispered. "It's only at night or if it rains that he gets really energetic."

Elodie nodded, remembering the speed at which Dash had thundered down her road.

"Where did you come from?" she murmured, holding out a handful of dandelion clocks.

Dash blinked at her quizzically and she felt her heart stirring with wonderment. In a single slow glide, Elodie stepped towards the magnificent unicorn and knelt before him, bowing her head in respect, her hair crackling.

"So this is Stormy's dad?" Marnie whispered in a voice as soft as mist. She still seemed a bit wary after being attacked by the baby unicorn.

Rufus slowly lumbered forwards, approaching the majestic beast, sniffing the cold air and then (quite unexpectedly) licking the unicorn's snow-white face.

Kit gave a small gasp of alarm, and Elodie stifled a giggle, but Dash hardly reacted other than to nuzzle the dog fondly.

"Dash is definitely Stormy's dad," announced Caleb. "Rufus knows. They must have the same scent."

"But if Dash has a baby, why aren't they together?" asked Rishi, looking puzzled.

"I think I know the answer to this," Kit said, taking his mum's phone from his pocket, feeling the familiar buzz of excitement he got when they discovered something new about unicorns. "Look at this letter Caleb and I found from the online archives of the Museum of Ice Explorers," he said proudly. "It states that Winter's Dawn unicorns retreat into the water as a way of staying safe. It's how they keep themselves hidden. Probably how they've survived all this time unseen."

They all studied the entry from Ava Bjornson.

"So Stormy's safer in the lake?" asked Caleb.

"Must be," agreed Marnie-Mae.

Elodie thought back to the moment she had seen Dash frantically charging down the street, and the terrifying jolt that had struck her when the van sped past. How she had just known that a unicorn was trapped inside, as Maman and Mrs Singh had.

"I think Dash is trying to keep Stormy hidden from the men in the van by separating himself from her," she explained as the others nodded.

"You've never seen Stormy here in the community garden, have you?" she asked Rishi.

"Nope. Never. I mean, I only found out unicorns were real last Friday. I'd be pretty stunned to see a baby one."

"But you've seen Dash in the park?" she asked Caleb, who nodded.

"Yes. I spotted him when Kit and I had our stargazing class. I think he visits Stormy at twilight."

"So maybe the men in the van don't know about Stormy!" cried Marnie, forgetting to be secretive. "Dash is protecting Stormy by leading the men away."

"Yes!" agreed Rishi. "I mean, why else would he hang out behind the recycling bins?"

"We need to know everything Dash does between twilight and midnight," said Kit, getting his pencil and notebook ready.

"Well," Rishi began, "Dash normally vanishes for an hour or so around twilight. Then he appears again. The van turns up when it's properly dark and they go on this massive chase."

"He must be visiting Stormy and then coming back to face the men in the van," Kit mumbled as he scribbled everything down.

"So we need to find out who those men are," said Marnie with determination.

"I'll try and keep watch here tonight," Rishi piped

up eagerly.

"I'll speak to Maman as soon as I'm home," said Elodie. "She might know something. Either way, we can keep watch from my flat in case Dash runs past again … see if we can spot who's in the van. Marnie, can you ask your mum if you can sleep over?"

"Sure can," said Marnie-Mae with a grin, high-fiving Elodie and doing a jazzy twirl on her wheels.

"We could try and convince our mum to bring us back here to keep watch with you, Rishi?" Kit hissed in a noisy whisper.

"Say that you're studying night-blooming flowers," suggested Rishi, gesturing to a neat flower bed full of white flowers whose petals were closed to the glare of the sun.

"Moonflowers or angels trumpets," cried Caleb, grinning. He seemed genuinely interested in the wondrous flowers. He nodded and turned in a quick glide on his blade as he raced off to ask his mum right that minute.

The plan worked out far better than any of them could have imagined.

Rishi's mum Anisha had already invited Kit,

Caleb, Sophia and Rufus for dinner. Rishi's dad was cooking and the two mums were going to do a moon meditation, giving the boys the perfect opportunity to sneak away.

The little group of friends said goodbye. Max had arrived to take Elodie and Marnie-Mae to the park where they would wait for Stormy to emerge from the lake in the hope that Dash would come and visit her. Kit, Caleb and Rufus headed to Rishi's flat to keep watch for the crucial moment Dash returned, so they could find out who was in the van.

Caleb and Rufus had dinner on Rishi's balcony to keep an eye on Dash as he dozed. Caleb made a rough sketch of him, whilst also watching the sleeping moonflowers (in which, as it happened, he had a genuine interest). He could not wait for them to wake.

"So unicorns have been here for all of time?" Rishi asked Kit as they sat on his bed. They'd told their mums they were gaming.

"Yes," Kit began to explain, "long ago there was an epic storm and nine children got stranded in nine different parts of the world with their horses. A wishing star fell from the clouds, splintering into nine gleaming pieces. Each child wished that their horse would not be harmed by the storm. And when lightning struck, every horse was marked for ever with a horn made of bone and starlight, and enchanted with the power of thunder."

"I would never have believed it five days ago." Rishi sighed. "But now..."

"And unicorns have always loved South London."

"Seriously?" said Rishi, laughing. "How do you know?"

"Princess Grace used to draw them. There's a whole selection of illustrations at the museum and in the Map of Lost Unicorns," said Kit, showing Rishi the photo of Princess Grace's drawings he'd saved on his mum's phone.

"That's incredible," Rishi muttered to himself.

This was still all so new to him. He hadn't dared tell any of his friends at school about Dash – he was sure they wouldn't believe him – and all of his friends that lived in his block were convinced Dash was a horse. It was so wonderful to have found friends who he could share this discovery with.

A whole new landscape of possibilities was opening up for Rishi. One filled with mystery and marvel and mythical beings hidden behind the recycling bins!

Twilight rolled in thick as wood-smoke, covering South London in a deep autumnal haze. In the stillness of Oak Grove community garden and the gentle chatter of the large leafy park, the five friends were ready.

Standing with Rishi on his little concrete balcony, Kit clutched his mum's phone, waiting with bated breath as they watched Caleb and Rufus below, poised near Dash. The phone pinged with a message from Marnie-Mae.

Stormy just came out of the lake like some sort of sassy siren-sea-horse. It was fabulous. And only me, Elle and a toddler spotted her. So we're cool.

Kit nodded to Rishi, and they turned to the seemingly docile unicorn below.

The moon hung in the night sky as Dash's blue eyes flashed open. From their position in the garden, Caleb leaned back and Rufus gave a little yelp of surprise as the unicorn leapt to his feet and gave a swish of his horn.

And then, as quietly as falling snow, Dash vanished into the crisp evening air.

Rufus gave a forlorn little howl and Caleb tenderly patted the dog's head. Rufus had become quite attached to the magnificent unicorn, it seemed.

Kit and Rishi joined Caleb in the community garden.

"So you reckon he's gone to visit Stormy?" asked Kit, checking Sophia's phone for another message from Marnie-Mae.

Caleb gave a very certain nod, and the phone pinged moments later. Kit read the message aloud.

Oh wow! Dash is here now, he just stepped out of the air like a prince of winter. I totally forgot they could do that! More soon!
   Mx

Kit and Rishi looked at each other, their eyes alight

with hope. Caleb grinned to himself and hugged Rufus. Now there was nothing to do but wait for Dash to return.

Eventually, when the luminous moon had risen and the sky had darkened to indigo, the next message from Marnie arrived.

Dash has left the lake shore! Repeat: Dash has left the lake shore. Expect a large moon-coloured unicorn, to reappear any sec—

"There!" cried Rishi, pointing to what looked like a small, shockingly bright firework lighting up the alleyway behind the recycling bins. There was a whirl of cold air and a small flurry of snow, then Dash stepped majestically from the night, as suddenly as he had departed.

At the exact same moment, to Caleb's delight, the little white moonflowers unfurled into dazzling star-shaped blooms, soaking up the moonlight and filling the night with the silky soft fragrance of midnight rain.

Caleb managed to pluck one just before Dash

stooped his head and devoured the little white buds.
Rufus gave a happy whimper, pleased to see his friend,
but Caleb gently hushed him, sensing the unicorn's
flighty energy.

Dash whinnied, his eyes alert as he strode

purposefully into the garden, circling around it once and coming to rest under the pear tree.

Suddenly, roaming headlights flooded the garden. The flowers curled their petals against the harsh, unwelcome light and the sound of violins filled the air, like a melody woven from silver.

"Get down! It's the van!" hissed Rishi, ducking behind a large bush. Kit quickly hid under the bench beneath the pear tree, and Caleb and Rufus snuck behind the recycling bins where Dash had just been hidden.

From their hiding places, they heard the sound of a door slamming and voices muttering in an unknown language.

Dash began pawing the ground with a huge, glassy hoof.

Caleb's heart was racing. He could feel the anxiety of the winter unicorn radiating through the dark. Rufus nestled into him, unnerved by the tension.

A furious banging roared from the van, as if someone had tried to contain thunder inside, and Kit, Rishi and Caleb all held their breath, knowing it must be the sound of a mother in distress.

The two men entered the garden. They had flashlights but didn't need them. The gleam of the moon lit their path and illuminated Dash like a horse cut from diamonds. He was striking by day, but by night Dash was sensational.

At the sight of the men, the unicorn reared up ferociously and a blizzard of sleet and hail tumbled fiercely from his hooves, stunning the two men, who drew back, shielding their faces.

In that moment, Dash charged straight at them, his horn pointed forward like a wild rhino.

Caleb covered his eyes.

Both men dived in opposite directions, falling in a heap on the dusty ground. But one of them leapt up and hurled a long, looped rope towards Dash. It was the electric blue of the sea light and held the crackle of storms.

"A lightning rope," gasped Kit. A net woven from lightning was the only thing that could capture a unicorn. Once the rope went over Dash's horn, he could never escape.

Kit knew the unicorn's only chance was to vanish into the air. It would only buy him so much time, as unicorns couldn't stay hidden for too long without re-emerging somewhere close by. It was more like they stepped into a little corridor of invisibility than actually vanished, but it might save Dash from the net. The men would no doubt track him, but at least he'd be free for now.

But Dash made no move to vanish.

"Maybe he doesn't want the men to know his secrets, in case he needs that trick another time?" Kit pondered, dropping his head in sorrow. Nothing he'd learned about unicorns could help him save Dash from a lightning rope. Rishi gazed on in horror from behind the bush. From within the little alleyway, Caleb peeked between his fingers and made a decision.

"Go, Rufus, go!" he urged.

The huge fluffy dog tore through the community garden, barrelling straight into the man clutching the lightning rope. The rope slipped from the man's hands and fell to the ground.

Using the distraction, Dash cleared the gate of the gardens in a single bound, and cantered away on pounding hooves.

A FINE DAY IN MAY
1500s. Gardens of the Palace of Crystal

Burning Sand Spells:
Desert unicorns
Sandy in colour, with creamy
manes, shire-horse hooves
and white horns.

Nightingale's Heart:
Forest unicorns
Deep chestnut-brown coats,
reddish manes, mossy green
hooves and amber horns.

Twilight Grace:
Mist/Rain unicorns
Grey, silver or white unicorns,
with lilac manes and irises.

Juniper Blue:
Valley unicorns
Often multi-coloured,
but with blue horns.

From the sketchbook of the Royal Princess Grace,
aged 11, listing the different types of unicorn.

Winter's Dawn:
Snow and ice unicorns
Entirely white with glassy
horns, frost-blue manes,
tails and hooves.

Surf Dancer:
Beach unicorns
Golden or pale brown, with
shell-pink hooves and horns,
and sea-foam manes.

Indigo River:
Water unicorns
Deepest black, indigo
mane, clear, ice-like horn
and hooves.

Cloud-spun Dreamer:
Mountain unicorns
White or grey, clompy
hooves, and wings!

The two men scrambled to their feet, grabbed the rope and retreated, swearing furiously at Rufus. A light clicked on and Sophia and Anisha appeared in the gardens looking highly irritated.

"That is no way to speak to a family pet!" said Sophia, marching towards the men.

"This garden is a place of peace. You are not welcome here if you can't keep to the rules," Anisha echoed, following behind.

To everyone's surprise, the men looked rather embarrassed and started apologizing, which gave Kit all the time he needed to text Marnie-Mae.

We've seen the men. Both tall – one ginger, one fair. My mum is currently telling them off for frightening Rufus! They have a lightning rope... Dash got away. I reckon he's on his way to you.

On the other side of the leafy park, in a little flat on the second floor, Marnie-Mae's phone pinged and it was time for action.

CHAPTER SEVEN
HOW TO SUMMON A UNICORN

Moonlight gathered in silver pools upon the carpet of the little second-floor flat as Elodie and Marnie-Mae crouched in the semi-darkness, studying the shadows in the lovely leafy park.

There was not a single light on in the entire flat, so it seemed from the outside as if everyone was sleeping.

Elodie's parents were in the kitchen quietly talking, the light of a candle flickering between them. As her dad brewed a strong pot of organic coffee, Maman tucked her glorious curls into a scarf, and all of them waited for a glimpse of the unicorn or the glaring headlights of the van, whichever came first.

Dash, hoped Elodie, wrapping her dressing gown more tightly around her.

Marnie-Mae had the camera open on her phone so she could film the van and zoom in to uncover who the strange unicorn hunters were. Elodie had her unicorn whistle around her neck: a special shell they'd acquired when they were rescuing Astra which could summon unicorns.

The two friends gazed into the night, hardly daring to breathe. Ever so softly, Elodie's curls began to zing, flickering with flecks of blue lightning.

"Dash must be near," Marnie mouthed, her brown eyes wide with excitement.

Elodie sat forward, her heart pounding like the hooves of a horse. But it was not the firm, fearless charging she was used to with Dash. It was chaotic and wild.

Maman moved swiftly from the kitchen, her coffee still in her hand, drawn to the window by the surge of energy she could also feel. Max was right behind her, his trusty pair of ancient binoculars looped around his neck.

As Elodie's curls rose into a crackling halo,

illuminating the room, everyone peeked around the curtain, pressing their faces to the misty glass.

Outside, the street was quiet. A few leaves danced in the lamplight and a city fox sauntered casually by. Something flashed in the park beyond.

Elodie and Marnie gripped each other's hands in wild hope. However, it was not the brilliant glare of a snowstorm they had been expecting. It was more like the radiance of a little star. The light gradually grew brighter, but it was irregular – sometimes flashing, sometimes vanishing for a few seconds.

"That's kind of random?" said Marnie in a low voice.

"No!" gasped Maman.

And all at once Elodie understood.

This was not the powerful racing of Dash, but the wild stamping of Stormy.

In a dazzle of luminous joy, the white foal came bounding over the park fence and leapt playfully on to the roof of a parked car. The car alarm blasted through the dark, making Max spill his coffee and Marnie shriek in shock. Elodie jumped in surprise and Maman said some bad words in French. Stormy clattered around on top of the car, like a little moon-kissed goat.

"What is she doing? We have to hide her," cried Maman in horror, as the wash of headlights approached the street corner.

But Elodie was already halfway across the room, racing out of the door, with Marnie-Mae at her heels, camera in hand.

They half tumbled, half slid down the stairs, years of skating making them hardy to falls. Elodie yanked the door open, the lamplit night whirling in as both girls rushed outside.

There was Stormy, mischievously prancing around on the cars..

"Stormy!" called Elodie, nervously holding out her arms.

Stormy stopped jumping and stared at Elodie, her horn glinting sharply in the dark. Elodie felt the pull of the little unicorn's thoughts like a bright light at the edge of her mind.

"You're safe with us," she murmured, willing Stormy to understand.

But Stormy whinnied and began galloping chaotically over other parked cars, a cacophony of alarms echoing through the night. Elodie raised the unicorn whistle to her lips and blew. It made a sound like a harp playing underwater and Stormy's horn flashed at the sound of it. Still, she did not move any closer to Elodie.

"What on earth is going on out there?" came a disgruntled voice from one of the flats further along the road. "Is that a feral deer?"

Elodie glanced anxiously at Marnie. "What do we do?" she mouthed.

Marnie-Mae stepped in front of Elodie into the spotlight of a street lamp and shook out her fabulous hot-pink braids.

"Come on, Stormy, let's play tag, " she called, her voice bright and happy.

And at once, like an arctic star drawn north, Stormy clattered off the car and charged at Marnie.

Elodie stumbled back as Marnie-Mae fled into the little flat and up the stairs to the second floor. Stormy tore after her like a bolt of lightning released from the clouds. Elodie heard a loud crash, her dad shouting, her maman crying out with joy and the beat of her racing heart.

She turned to step inside the little flat and close its

bright blue door, escaping the gaze of the befuddled neighbours, who were all trying to silence their car alarms. But the beating of her heart only quickened, and Elodie realized with a startled gasp that Dash was still out there. She pulled the door half closed, leaving just enough space to peek out of.

Everyone will only think he's a horse, she reassured herself, as the clatter of hooves grew nearer.

For a moment she saw him, soaring magnificently down the street, his hooves and horn like mountain ice, his heart wild with fury. Elodie threw the door wide open and ran on to the pavement. The night suddenly became brighter than day and she closed her eyes, feeling a rush of grace and power brush past her.

Moments later everything went dark. The street lamps flickered out and the lights of a van faded from view. The silvery swirl of muted violins threaded their way through the air.

"Slow down! This is a residential street!" someone yelled.

Without stopping, the van snaked away from the road, which was now full of angry neighbours.

Elodie sighed with relief, her hair still crackling. Dash had got away ... and Stormy was safely inside. She closed the bright blue door and padded softly up the stairs, hoping that Dash had found somewhere to hide, or could outrun the van.

Back inside, Elodie stepped over the shattered pieces of a coffee cup and a spilled vase of lilies to discover both of her parents squeezed into the tiny bathroom, where a grinning Marnie-Mae sat in her pyjamas in a bath full of water with Stormy. Elodie chuckled softly. It's a most unexpected sight to find your best friend in the bath with a baby unicorn – even for a Unicorn Seeker.

Stormy was much calmer in the water, her head resting on the side of the bath, her beautiful horn twinkling as softly as starlight.

"She is quite something," said Maman in a low voice. "Even I have never seen a baby before. We will have to do everything we can to protect her."

Elodie nodded, still mesmerized by the nearness of the little mythical creature.

"We'll have to get her to safety in the morn—" began Elodie's dad when there came a knock at the door.

They all glanced at each other through the moonlit dark.

"It's probably just a neighbour who can't turn off their car alarm," said Max, gently pulling the shower curtain around Marnie-Mae and the baby unicorn, before closing the bathroom door to check.

Mrs Singh stood in the corridor, looking rather jolly.

"Hello," said Max kindly.

"Hello," Mrs Singh said with a smile. "There's a rather large unicorn in my flat eating all my herbs."

Max blinked in surprise and Maman came bursting out of the bathroom.

"Dash! Elle thinks that's his name," she said keenly. "Dash is here?"

Mrs Singh nodded. "I think so, yes."

"Bring him up at once!" Maman grinned.

"Thank you. Thank you so much. He really is rather large and nosy and ... well ... wild."

Twenty minutes later, when the moon dial clock showed a quarter to eleven, Marnie-Mae, Elodie, Maman and the two unicorns were squeezed precariously into Elodie's lounge.

Max, who was not quite able to see the luminous glitter of Dash's mythical horn, was staying safe in the kitchen, making more coffee and an awful lot of sandwiches. Marnie-Mae was perched by the window in some of Elodie's pyjamas, her braids wrapped up in a towel so she didn't lose any more to Stormy. Elodie sat cross-legged on the floor between Dash (who was curled dragon-like in the middle of the room) and Stormy (who was sleeping, stretched out like a cat upon the sunflower rug).

"Where have you come from?" Elodie whispered as she snuggled in close to Dash, careful not to wake Stormy.

Dash gazed at her with a look as fierce as fire, and Elodie knew – as she had with Astra – that she would go to the ends of the earth to keep Dash and his family safe. She was a Unicorn Seeker and just like her friends, protecting unicorns was her destiny.

Maman had been talking on the phone in a low secretive voice, her French too fast for Elodie to understand. She said farewell and turned to address the room importantly.

"I have spoken with my network and none of us know who the men in the van are, nor whom they work for. But," she continued, her eyes gleaming encouragingly, "we do know they are from Scandinavia, the same place that Dash's glory is from."

Marnie-Mae began fidgeting. She was desperate to phone Kit. He had done loads of research on Winter's Dawns, and she was sure she'd had some entries on the blog from people who lived in Sweden. But Esme was still speaking in a stirring tone which Marnie could not interrupt.

"The strange thing is," Maman explained, "there have been sightings of unicorns all over Scandinavia, particularly Norway, so we wondered why these men would bother to pursue a Winter's Dawn across Europe instead of hunting for one at home."

Elodie's heart fluttered softly with dread.

"It's Stormy," she whispered. "They are trying to capture Stormy."

"Yes," said Maman, with a heavy sigh.

Marnie put her hands over her mouth in horror. "But why?" she gasped.

"A horn can be used for many things," Maman said slowly. "Cloud cutting, curing sickness. It can be sprinkled over soup to make you look younger, its powder can heal any scar if mixed with nettle and lemon balm. And if sipped at a full moon it's said to reveal the future. But a baby unicorn's horn is even more powerful, more potent. Who knows what magic it might have!"

Dash gave a sudden whinny and they all stared at this blissfully innocent baby, peacefully dreaming.

Marnie-Mae seized Elodie's hand. "Well, we're going to stop anything bad from happening to her. All of us!" she said with firm defiance. "We'll free Stormy's mum and get all of them to safety!"

"Exactly," said Max, coming out of the kitchen with a huge pile of sandwiches. "It's time for another road trip."

Elodie and Marnie locked eyes with delight, and Maman smiled proudly at the two hopeful Unicorn Seekers.

"We leave tonight."

CHAPTER EIGHT
LATE NIGHT ESCAPE

At six minutes to midnight, as the moon illuminated the London sky, Elodie, Max, Esme and Marnie tiptoed into the park, along with two frost-coloured unicorns.

Dash regally led the way, trampling daisies and dandelions as he went. Elodie crept behind him, clutching her pink suitcase. Marnie followed and Stormy pranced along quite happily between her and Max and Maman.

When they reached the Feather and Fern, a small whispering group had gathered, just as they'd asked them to. Joni (Marnie-Mae's mum) was standing next to the van, wearing a nightdress, puffer jacket and Ugg boots. Next to her, Sophia was sitting on the damp grass in her yoga gear, holding Rufus' lead as Kit and Caleb glided around her in pyjamas and roller skates. Elodie smiled at her two friends. Kit grinned back at her, raising his hand in a wave, but Caleb stared at the ground and kept skating in a small loop, the motion of the wheels helping to calm him. Elodie knew he felt deeply concerned for Stormy and was trying to prepare for what would happen next.

"What's going on?" asked Joni, staring in alarm at the two brilliant white horses before her.

"Who do these horses belong to?" asked Sophia, curiously.

Maman spoke gently. "Joni, Sophia, your children – as we know – are wonderful young people. But they are also keen-hearted, courageous protectors of endangered animals."

Elodie stared nervously at Maman, knowing that the world was about to change for her friends' mums. It felt terrifying and exciting all at once. She smiled at Marnie-Mae, who looked just as nervous. She turned her gaze to Kit and Caleb – they'd texted to try to forewarn them. Kit gave her a grin of understanding, but Caleb was silent and worried.

"Yes, but why've you called us here in the middle of the night?" snapped Joni, looking confused. "Are these horses endangered?"

"These aren't ordinary horses," said Maman carefully. "They're unicorns."

Sophia blinked in surprise and Joni rolled her eyes, letting everyone know she was not in the mood for midnight pranks.

"It's true, Mum," said Marnie desperately. "Look, we'll show you."

Elodie stepped between the two unicorns, closed her eyes and prepared to lay her hands upon them both, so that just for a moment, the others might catch a flicker of their horns.

"No," said Caleb very firmly. "We promised not to tell anyone about Stormy... You all promised to keep her safe."

Maman, who had known Caleb since he was very young, approached him gently.

"It's all right, Caleb. I know you take your gift very seriously. But if we don't help Stormy, those men will catch her and kill her. We'll need your help to separate Dash and Stormy, take them both to safety and rescue Stormy's mum. To do that, though, we need your mum's permission."

Caleb was still as he considered this. He softened from furious to anxious as he weighed the risk of telling their mums with the need to protect the unicorns.

"Not Stormy. Only Dash," he said after a little while, and Elodie understood.

She turned to face Dash and stroked his long velvety nose. Suddenly the night was brighter than a firework shot through with rainbow sparks, and standing before them was a unicorn of moon-bright magnificence.

Both mums gasped.

Dash's coat seemed paler than the last star of morning, his tail and mane aglow like stardust, his hooves opaque and his horn as sharp and dazzling as diamonds.

Elodie let go, and Dash looked, once more, like a horse.

Joni was speechless and Sophia was dabbing tears from her eyes.

"Elodie and I come from a long line of seekers,"

explained Esme. "It is our duty to protect unicorns. We must get these two out of London and to do that, we will need everyone's help."

Joni and Sophia could hardly argue. So, in the shadow of a large oak tree, where the tropical parakeets lived, in the lovely leafy park, a midnight plan was made.

Elodie, Max, Marnie-Mae and Stormy would travel in the Feather and Fern to Reykjavik in Iceland to find a retired member of Esme's network who lived there: the world-famous harpist, Silke Andersdotter. Iceland was full of its own wild horses, and though Winter's Dawns didn't usually dwell there, Maman was sure that Stormy would fit right in. Sophia, Kit and Caleb would escort Dash back to Norway. If the men in the van were after a baby, Dash would be safer far away from Stormy and back with his glory.

This left Esme, who would remain in London to try and discover who the men were and work out how to set Stormy's mum free.

"I'll need to speak to your friend Rishi first thing in the morning," said Maman in a serious tone.

"I'll text him now," said Kit. "Rishi discovered Dash. Without his help, we could never have done any of this."

"Thank you, Kit," said Maman kindly. "I'll also speak to Mrs Singh and see if she knows anything about Stormy's mother."

"As I said on the phone, I'll have to stay behind and work. But let me know if there's anything I can do to help," offered Joni. Her career was of the utmost importance to her, but if she was going to support her beautiful Marnie-Mae in saving unicorns, then she would do everything she could to encourage and provide for her.

A midnight owl swooped over the moonlit lake and Max checked his watch.

"We'd better be going," he said excitedly.

Esme rested her forehead delicately against Dash's, just beneath his horn. Dash closed his eyes and the unicorn and the seeker were both quiet for some time. Everyone watched in spellbound wonder.

Then, with a deep breath, they both stepped away from each other. The unicorn reared up quite spectacularly before lowering his horn and approaching Stormy. Stormy became serious and raised her horn to meet her father's, like two crossed swords. And even though Sophia and Joni could not quite see the glinting magic of the horns, they were moved by the love and power between the two unicorns.

"Dash understands they must be parted," said Esme a little sorrowfully. Everyone sadly smiled and hugged goodbye.

Kit, Caleb and Sophia set off home with Rufus and Dash to figure out the details of their trip to Norway. None of them had ever travelled with a horse – let alone a unicorn – but Kit was sure it could be done. They would just need to find a ferry that allowed animals onboard.

Maman and Max carefully guided an energetic Stormy into the back of the coffee van. Elodie and Marnie-Mae clambered giddily in behind her. Elodie was amazed at how spacious it seemed. Stormy was much smaller (though less tame) than Astra had been. There was plenty of room for Elodie's pink suitcase and both girls' roller skates.

"Take care, *ma cherie*," said Maman, hugging

Elodie. Elodie smiled back. She did not feel sad to be parted from Maman this time, not the way she used to. Saving unicorns was her destiny, and they both understood the importance of the mission.

"Goodbye, you wonderful unicorn savers. I love you!" called Joni, leaning into the van to plant a big kiss on Marnie's cheek.

"It's seekers, Mum! We're Unicorn Seekers!" Marnie laughed before Max closed the van doors, climbed in and turned on the engine as quietly as possible. The luminous green van roared to life and

began to snake its way out of the park, headed for the coast.

In the back of the van, Elodie and Marnie-Mae stared at each other in a swirl of heart-stopping joy. They had not had a proper adventure like this since they discovered Astra. This was going to be the best weekend ever!

"Stormy is truly unique," breathed Marnie, ducking out of the unicorn's way as Elodie tried to soothe the little beast. Stormy was not very keen on the motion of the van and couldn't seem to settle. Her hooves kept striking out and knocking over the smoothie maker and stacks of recycled paper cups. Elodie's heart felt the rattle and pull of the unicorn's panic, so she did what Maman used to do when she was little and couldn't sleep. She began to softly sing a French lullaby.

Eventually, Stormy curled up – half on Elodie and half on top of the fridge – and as Elodie stroked her mane, she was surprised to find the little unicorn felt cool to the touch.

As the van hurtled along the motorway, all three of them drifted into a deep sleep.

Elodie dreamed of snow and a deep green sea. She dreamed she was standing upon an iceberg, floating and bobbing like a little ship. The wild sea was dotted with other icebergs, all glistening in the soft twilight. And upon the largest iceberg was a lighthouse, casting out a single ghostly beam. In the distance she saw Stormy standing on a little raft of ice. In her sleep Elodie smiled.

Stormy raised her gleaming horn and shook out her luminous mane. All at once, Elodie heard music, the song of waves and sea. Stormy launched herself off the raft and dived deep beneath the surface of the sea, swimming as if she were running through the waves. And all around her the water shimmered and sparkled, and for a moment it seemed as if the little horse was covered in scales that glimmered and glowed like moonlight.

Down she dived, the song of water singing in her heart, a world of mermaids and merrows waiting to welcome her. In her dream, Elodie gasped with joy, for she knew that the little unicorn belonged in this underwater kingdom.

The Nordic Sea, 1989

From the deck of the Sea Iris,
beneath a guiding star.

My dearest Silke,

Gosh how you would adore it here. The waves are rough and the wind is fierce and the salt is true. But in the moments between storms, when the sea is calm and kissed by moonlight, I often think of you. It reminds me so much of our childhood, how you used to believe that the moon was lighting a path for us, and if we followed it, we would sail all the way to somewhere magical.

And you were right, my darling sister. Three nights ago, after I'd eaten a supper of boiled frankfurters, with baked beans and rye bread — and of course, a little bit of pickled shark — I found I could not sleep. There were no storms, just stillness, and even though there were no other boats in sight, I was certain I heard music. Not by any voice nor instrument I could name, more like a song made from water, calling in the voice of the sea. I peered over the side of the deck and saw a pale light deep underwater. It was unlike anything I've ever seen. Similar to the radiance of a blue whale, but bright as a star.

What strange creature could this be? It seemed to be drawn to moonlight.

The hour was late, but I knew I had to follow it. And so I sailed the path of the moon, Silke, and you will not believe what I found! A place where winter seemed eternal, ice-floats scattering the sea. Upon one island was a lighthouse, pale as bone. And beneath the water, a herd of magnificent white horses swimming as swiftly as dolphins. At first, I thought I must be dreaming, but as one of them crested the waves, its mane the ice-blue of the mountains, its coat so pearly it was almost scale-like, I'm sure that behind its ears I saw gills.

It dipped down beneath the water. Quickly, I seized my torch and used the light to draw the miraculous creature back to the side of the boat. Only this time, when it broke the surface, I saw that it was not a horse at all, but a unicorn with a horn as clear as ice.

A streak of lightning split the sky and I had to take cover, but in that moment, Silke, I remembered. I remembered the time we saw a unicorn as children when we were staying with our grandma in Norway.

And so, my beloved sister, I am writing to tell you that we were right. There have always been unicorns in the world and now that I have discovered these water-dwelling beauties, I will follow them for as long as I have life left to live.

All my love,

Ingrid

CHAPTER NINE

THE CALL OF THE WATER

Elodie awoke to find Marnie-Mae chuckling as she fed Stormy a handful of blueberry muffin crumbs. She sat up and stretched. But her eyes were watering, her nose was running, and her skin felt clammy and she could not stop shivering. She glanced at the moon dial clock, which was wedged on top of the coffee machine. It said seven a.m. They'd been on the road for seven hours! Only it didn't feel as if they were on the road: the van kept lurching and tipping.

"Where are we, Dad?" Elodie said as she coughed. Her throat felt so dry.

"Oh, great, you're awake." Max beamed. "We're on the way to Reykjavik on a trade ship!"

Both girls' mouths fell open in surprise.

"There aren't any ferries to Iceland, so we had to catch a freight ship from Southampton."

"Cool!" cried Marnie, opening the curtains of the van.

Beyond the rusted rails of the ship, she could see the crashing waves of a wild autumn sea.

Stormy gave a wild neigh, reared up and dented the roof of the van with her horn. Elodie shivered hard and pressed her hands together.

"You don't look so great, Elle," said Marnie-Mae as she handed Elodie a chocolate croissant.

Elodie took a bite and felt sick. "It was my dream. It was like a vision," she replied, opening her pink suitcase and taking out the silver tub with the beautiful winged horse embossed on the lid. With the gentlest care Elodie opened the pot. At once the van filled with a scent so wonderful that the day felt bright with hope. First came the aroma of rain on a midsummer eve. Then the rushing saltiness of the sea. Followed by the swift scent of frost. Lastly, the smell of moonlight descended upon the entire van. Elodie felt instantly better, yet the image of the bone-white lighthouse stayed with her.

Stormy was delighted as she breathed in the aroma of moonlight, her eyes burning a bold sapphire blue and her horn aglow.

"She's incredible," Marnie whispered, risking giving the little unicorn a super-light hug. "And she's freezing cold! Like a penguin or a whale. Not that I've ever hugged a whale."

"I think Stormy belongs in the water," said Elodie slowly. "Like when she hid in the lake… I just had a dream that she was swimming deep underwater."

"OK, we'd better keep her inside the van. I'm not going in after her if she dives overboard!"

"I'll stay with her," said Elodie, feeling slightly sick again at the rocking of the waves.

Marnie-Mae and Max squeezed outside to breathe in the salty sea air, while Elodie and Stormy hung their heads out of the van's small window, laughing as sea spray splashed their faces.

The morning passed slowly, the ship bobbing and swaying across the deep swirling sea, and Elodie let the memory of her dream fade away.

When she was back inside, Marnie-Mae's phone pinged with a text from Kit:

Hey! How's it going?

Dash has settled in well to our greenhouse. Caleb and I camped in there with him overnight. It was super cool. He didn't leave once, and there's no sign of the van so far. Not even a hint of the violins they're always playing.

We're just packing to leave for Norway. We found a ferry that lets horses and dogs onboard, but we have to travel below deck. Caleb's not feeling great about it. He thinks it'll be like in the Titanic. But he's super excited about seeing a blue whale, so I'm hoping we do see one and that that gets him through. See ya! Kit

"Land ahoy!" called Max in his best pirate voice.

Marnie-Mae gave a shriek of excitement and ran to the rails. Elodie raised her hand to her brow to peer into the mist through the little window and Stormy looked up enthusiastically.

Gradually, a little harbour came into view. It was

bustling with people and seabirds circled above.

"This place looks awesome!" Marnie whooped.

And she was right, there was something truly magical about it. The way the air felt full of salt and stories, and the sun was as pale as the moon. The bright joy of Reykjavik nipped at Elodie's heart. Even Stormy was enchanted.

The harbour was technically for tourists and fishermen, but Max managed to quickly drive the Feather and Fern into the streets of the little city without too much bother. They parked on a side street near a natural hot spa and very carefully let Stormy out of the van. The plan was to head to the concert hall on foot and find Silke, hoping that the people they passed would be charmed by a lively little horse. Elodie was worried Stormy might bolt, or start leaping over cars again, and she clutched her unicorn whistle in her hand. But the little foal was obediently calm, as if just being near the icy sea, volcanic mountains and lava fields was enough to soothe her.

Getting through town was slightly trickier. Stormy was fascinated by everything. First, she ran into an expensive clothes shop and came out munching a bobble hat. Then she charged into a cafe and devoured a pot of chocolate sauce. Before anyone could stop her, she leapt at a life-size statue of a polar bear outside the Viking museum, knocking it to the ground.

"Lucky we've got our roller skates," gasped Marnie-Mae, trying not to laugh as Elodie struggled to catch up with the unicorn. Thankfully, everyone seemed quite bewitched by the little white horse, even letting her keep the bobble hat. Max was very relieved indeed.

Finally, after Stormy had extinguished every candle in a quaint wintry church by swishing her fabulous tail, munched on a florist's prized winter camelias and knocked over a collection of yellow bicycles, they reached a sweeping green lake. Elodie threw her arms around Stormy's neck as the little unicorn's eyes glowed brighter than stars, her horn glittering, heart racing.

"You can't go in right now, Stormy," Elodie whispered, pressing her forehead to Stormy's just below her horn and trying to communicate with her thoughts.

Stormy stamped her glassy hoof crossly and Elodie felt the tug of the water, calling to Stormy like the song from her dreams. She was desperately torn between keeping Stormy safe and giving her what she craved. The watery depths of the lake were too much, and the little unicorn broke free of Elodie's grasp, her glowing horn grazing Elodie's cheek.

Max swore and Marnie-Mae screamed.

A group of teenage girls who were posing for a group selfie were completely photo-bombed by Stormy and began howling with laughter and filming her. A man who was fishing began yelling his disapproval in Icelandic.

"Look! A unicorn!" said a little girl on the other side of the lake, pointing in astonishment.

Panic swept over Elodie. Stormy was drawing too much attention!

"We've got to call her back!" cried Marnie. "If that video goes viral, the men in the van will find out where she is."

"Elle, use the whistle," urged Max, running down to the shore.

Elodie raised the shell to her lips and blew, the notes ringing out in a melody just for Stormy. For a moment, Elodie sensed Stormy's hesitation. But the pull of the water was too great. Stormy could not resist the wild depths of the lake. It was where she belonged.

With a tearful gasp, Elodie closed her eyes, letting her hair crackle fiercely, drawing the elements to her. Her love for Stormy and the wild energy of her electric-blue curls felt overwhelming. All at once, the sky switched from palest grey to thunderous black, and the air cracked with the surge of a storm. Rain shot down swift as arrows, drumming on the surface of the water. People shrieked and fled to shelter, paying no more attention to the little white horse as she plunged into the lake and vanished with a mermaid's grace.

Elodie's hair rose around her and she felt as if she herself was the storm. Lightning zapped from the sky, zinging through her hair and, suddenly exhausted, Elodie stumbled. Marnie-Mae and Max took hold of her hands, carefully guiding her to the nearest bench.

"That was incredible," whispered Marnie, as the rain pattered around them. "You totally caused a storm."

"Not even your mum can draw rain from the sky," said Max fondly, stroking Elodie's scratched cheek.

"Stormy belongs underwater," Elodie explained as she got her breath back.

Max and Marnie-Mae nodded their understanding, and together they made their way around the lake towards the Harpa Concert Hall.

"So Stormy can live underwater like a mermaid?" asked Marnie-Mae excitedly.

"Maman was certain Winter's Dawns only hide in the water, not live there," Max said as they approached the entrance.

"And Kit reckoned the same from some documents he read online," added Marnie.

"Not always," came a gentle voice, and they all turned to see a woman with hair the silver-white of starlight and a warm sun-kissed face, holding a yellow umbrella and a large, elegant case. By the shape of it, Elodie was sure it must contain a harp.

"You must be Silke?" Max grinned and held out a hand, which Silke firmly shook.

"You'd better come with me, and I will tell you all I know."

★

As evening fell, they all sat together in the cafe on the third floor of the concert hall, gazing over the lake to keep a close eye out for any sign of Stormy.

Silke's harp case was standing in the corner, and she clasped a steaming cup of black coffee in both hands. Everyone else swigged fresh sparkling spring water and ate smoke salmon on crackers. All around them floated notes of music: fragments of melodies and snippets of haunting harmonies being rehearsed on a stage just out of sight. Elodie felt completely soothed by it.

"One thing is for certain," said Silke with genuine concern, "Stormy can't stay with me as I'd hoped. I saw what happened out there. She is too wild. Too visible. People will notice her."

Elodie nodded, feeling crestfallen. "Where can we take her so she'll be safe?"

"I might know of a place," said Silke gently. They all leaned forward. "I am not a seeker myself, but my brilliant sister Ingrid was, and I sometimes glimpsed them when I was with her. Ever since she disappeared, I have been helping other seekers in any way I can."

"Disappeared?" asked Max.

"Ingrid vanished at sea many years ago. Perhaps her boat sank, perhaps she fell in love with a merman, or perhaps she is still out there somewhere. This is the last letter I have from her."

Silke handed them the sea-stained letter, worn thin by the wind, but still just about readable.

"So there *are* underwater unicorns! Do you think they've adapted? Like grown gills and stuff?" chattered Marnie-Mae.

"That lighthouse was in my dream," said Elodie softly.

The whole table turned to stare at her. Silke's eyes had become misted with hope.

"I think this sea that your sister speaks of is where Stormy belongs," said Elodie. "If we could just find a way to get her there, she'd be safe."

"We'd need to sail the path of the moon," said Max a little doubtfully. "I'm not much of a sailor but…"

"I am, though. And I do have a small boat," said Silke, a deep warmth radiating from her as she sipped her coffee. "It is the last known place my sister visited. I should like to see it. We can leave as soon as the moon is fully risen."

Beyond the window, the October sky had darkened to deepest indigo, dotted with arctic stars. Soon the lake had become deserted as people hurried home for tea. "I guess we'd better try to summon Stormy again," said Elodie, not at all sure how it would go.

Together they headed to the lake shore. Most of the water birds seemed to be settling in for the night, out of the light patter of rain. Elodie clutched her unicorn whistle and softly blew the pink shell. At first all was still. They waited, counting heartbeats until with a splash Stormy reared out of the water and came cantering joyously towards them.

"Move!" yelled Max, pulling the others out of the

way as Stormy's hooves churned up a spray of little black rocks. But Stormy was so ecstatic to see them all that Elodie and Marnie, and even Silke didn't mind the odd scratch of her horn, or stamp on their toes, as Stormy danced around them.

"It's going to be a long night." Max sighed as they wound their way through the twinkly streets of Reykjavik. Soon they would sail the path of the moon. But for now, they were going to have dinner and a shower at Silke's house and prepare for the next night of their adventure.

An illustration of Nordessa the Mer-Horse, from the Scandinavian folktale Merchild and her horses.

Long ago in the deep seas of Nordica, lived a Merchild who wished to travel on land. Everyone forbade it for the Mer did not trust the humans. But the Merchild was wilful and brave, and she turned her flock of sea horses into land horses, so they might carry her to the surface and beyond, whenever she so wished.

It is said that her most trusted horse, Nordessa, was also a unicorn, living both on land and beneath the waves of the crashing sea.

CHAPTER TEN

THE VIOLA IN THE VAN

On a ferry upon the Nordic Sea, Kit, Caleb, Sophia, Rufus and a surprisingly docile Dash were nestled below deck as the night rolled on, full of lightning and bursts of thunder.

Caleb had his back to the little round window which looked out over the swirling sea. Sophia had walked around the deck with him, so they knew where the lifeboats were placed – just in case – which had made the journey seem much more bearable. But he preferred not to look at the sea.

He sat in between Rufus and a snoozing Dash, a big chunky scarf wrapped over his nose to block out the damp smell of the cabin, distracting himself from the journey by doing further research on his iPad.

Caleb had always loved Nordic myths, especially the lesser-known ones. Since he'd learned that unicorns were real (not that he'd ever really doubted it), Caleb had been sure there were many other marvels just waiting to be discovered. And soon enough he found something mesmerizing. An image of a unicorn called Nordessa which lived out at sea.

"Hey, look," Caleb said when Sophia's phone pinged. He read the message from Rishi over Kit's shoulder.

Hi guys.

Elodie's maman came over to speak with my mum, and said she needed my help to track some "horse" smugglers.

My mum's properly cross at those men in the van because they've driven over half the community garden, so she totally agreed.

Now we're all crouched behind the recycling bins having a chai latte and waiting for the van to arrive. No sign of them yet, but I'll keep you posted.

Whatever happens we're going to set the captured unicorn free. I just know we are. Esme's got a cool plan. It's risky but I think it'll work.

P.S. Any tips for keeping unicorns calm, let me know!

Kit grinned at Caleb but Caleb didn't smile back. He felt worried for Rishi – he was new to unicorn seeking, and part of Caleb wished he could be there to help. What if something went wrong and Stormy's mum got hurt, or Rishi…

He began composing a message of support in his head when Dash's ice-blue eyes blinked open and darted around the room. Caleb leaned back in alarm, out of reach of Dash's sharp horn, as the unicorn abruptly rose to his feet. Sophia dropped her book in surprise, while Rufus lurched on to Kit's lap to either protect him, or be protected – it was hard to know. Dash gave a swift whinny and loud stamp, as if he was listening to something the others could not hear.

"What do we do?" asked Sophia.

Caleb stood up slowly and ever so gently reached out a palm to rest on Dash's neck, letting the unicorn's thoughts come to him. He felt Dash's consciousness like a light at the edge of his heart. First came the pull of the water with its deep and dazzling depths. Then the vastness of his love for Stormy and his unicorn family. And there was something else, threaded through all of it, that felt familiar to Caleb. Like a melody sewn from silver.

And then he knew.

"Music," said Caleb in a serious tone. "Dash can hear music."

"How lovely," said Sophia, looking relieved.

"No," said Caleb, shaking his head.

"Why? What's wrong with the music?" asked Kit, suspiciously, listening hard but not hearing anything. Last summer on a bridge in Prague all the Unicorn Seekers had almost fallen under the spell of a peculiar celloist. They certainly didn't want a repeat of that.

"Tell us what's up with the music?" Kit urged as he and Sophia strained to hear anything.

But Caleb couldn't answer. He wasn't sure. He just knew that he'd heard that melody before and it reminded him of danger.

Dash had started to pace, his stardust tail flicking from side to side, his eyes glowing with sapphire magnificence. Kit frowned and texted Marnie-Mae and Rishi the update.

Over the crashing waves of the sea, inland from the coast, south of the misty river, a little way from the lovely leafy park, behind the recycling bins of an award-winning community garden, Rishi's mum's phone buzzed. Esme frowned as she read the message.

"I wonder what sort of music a horse could hear in the middle of the sea?" pondered Anisha, quite unaware that Dash was a unicorn.

Time ticked by and they sipped their chai. The moonflowers opened into bright white angels' trumpets and night birds called sweetly. Then slowly came the low sound of wheels over tarmac, along with the hum of violin music as the lights of a vehicle roamed smoothly around the garden.

"That's the van," Rishi whispered and Esme nodded.

This time there was no frantic pounding from within. The two men did not get out, but parked in a corner of the garden, wound down the window and let the silvery soft melody spill into the night. Rishi listened hard. It was the same familiar classical tune the men were always playing. It was beautiful, like a song you might sing underwater, yet it felt so close, as if it was being performed inside the van.

Above them the clouds scattered in the skies, revealing a warm autumn moon, which lit the Oak Grove community garden in a gleaming gold. Rishi gave a little gasp. By the light of the moon, through the van's open window, he spied the man with the ginger beard playing an instrument similar to a violin only bigger.

"He's playing a viola," breathed Esme.

"Well, he's certainly very gifted," said Anisha. "The tune's so calming I could drift off to sleep."

"That's how they're keeping the captured horse calm," Esme explained, winking at Anisha and Rishi to signal that it was time to put the first step of their plan into action.

Esme stood up, watering can in hand and a raincoat thrown over her nightdress, its hood pulled up over her amazing curls. She began to casually hum, pretending to water the moonflowers.

The viola wavered, and the van engine revved.

"Oh, please don't stop playing. It's ever so soothing!" she cooed in a posh voice that made Rishi want to giggle. "I know it's a little late to be gardening," Esme chirruped on, "but you see, there's this lovely white horse that comes by around midnight. I think he must belong to a local city farm. Anyway, these little moonflowers are his favourite food – they grow all over the garden."

The viola paused as the blonde man clambered keenly out of the van. Then the song began again, the ginger bearded man still sweetly playing, as if trying to summon Dash from across the city.

Too late, thought Rishi gleefully, *Dash has escaped.*

As Elodie's maman distracted the blonde man by showing him the flowers, Rishi and his mum stealthily approached the van. They crept to the back doors and pressed their ears to the metal but heard no sound from within. Rishi closed his eyes and sighed. There at the edge of his mind he sensed the mother unicorn's power, bright as a star and full of feral dreams.

"I think she's asleep," he mouthed to Anisha, who nodded and reached for a golden locket which hung around her neck. It was heart-shaped and studded with tiny jewels, and as it clicked open, Rishi saw that concealed inside one half of the heart was a very small, very sharp key.

Rishi beamed. It was no secret that Anisha was an incredible jewellery maker and skilled locksmith. Delicately she slipped the key from the locket and with the utmost care, slotted it into the lock on the van door. There was a click, as soft as the flutter of a wing, then another one, slightly louder, like the snapping of fingers. And then with a whirring of clockwork, the key slowly turned and the doors opened.

In a heartbeat the savagely beautiful unicorn woke up. Rishi gasped in awe. She was fierce as a snow leopard, her coat the white of arctic winters, her mane and tail the blue of deep oceans, her hooves and horn crystal clear. All around her crackled a net made of lightning, restricting her movements, its electric blue light filling the garden like a firework.

"What on earth is that?" muttered Anisha.

"It's a really special horse, Mum," Rishi tried to assure her. "See how they've trapped her?"

The viola screeched to a halt. The blonde man abandoned the moonflowers and came running over, bellowing. The man with the ginger beard scrambled out of the van in a panic.

Rishi hugged his mum, took a breath and hopped into the back of the van, sliding past the fearsome unicorn and the sparking net and hiding in the shadows at the back. The plan had worked so far!

He just had to really hope his mum could pull off the next bit.

Anisha gave a worried gasp but nodded, then slammed the door shut and started yelling at the two men. "How dare you disturb the peace in our garden! What have I told you about being respectful? And what kind of creature have you got in there? I should call the RSPCA."

The two men began backing away from Anisha, mumbling apologetically. One of them tried to calm Anisha down while the other tried desperately not to engage. In all the commotion they did not notice Esme Lightfoot, true to her name, creep around to the front of the van and jump in. There was a startling burst of light as the engine flared to life, and then the grey van was racing off into the night. The two men spun around in shock and began to chase after it on foot. All Esme heard was an awful lot of shouting, and a word being repeated over and over: "Viola! Viola!"

She glanced down and was surprised to see that the bearded man had left his gleaming viola and bow on the passenger seat. Behind her, in the deep dark of the back of the van, Rishi took a breath and sat down on the floor, crossing his legs in the lotus position, just like his mum did when she was meditating. The mother unicorn pawed the ground hotly, but she did not come near him. Rishi noticed she had little singe marks all over her from where she'd been straining to break free of the net. He closed his eyes and sent a beat of love from his heart to hers. Gently, like a leaf afloat on the river, a name came to him.

"Lumi," Rishi whispered, turning to stare at her.

She met his gaze with her crystal-blue stare, as wild and glorious as glaciers and moonlight. Rishi felt a deep affinity with her, as he had with Dash. As if all of time had stopped, and all that mattered was setting this magical creature free.

We will help you.

He sent his thoughts to her, but she only glared at him silently.

At the wheel, Esme was taking them straight out of London and down to the coast where they could board a ship to Iceland. There was only one person who could free a unicorn from a lightning net and it was Esme's beloved daughter.

Anisha met them at Southampton Harbour. "I chased those two bandits as far away as I could!" she said proudly, parking her car and climbing into the van beside Esme. As she lifted the shining viola off the seat, an inscription caught her eye.

"With love from Madame de Souza," Anisha read as Esme drove on to the boat with the rusty railings.

"It means nothing to me," said Esme, "but let's text Max and Silke. They might know something."

But the message wouldn't send.

"They must have no signal," said Rishi as the boat set sail over the dark night sea.

The two mums were still in their pyjamas but they hardly cared. Anisha had managed to bring some chai latte in her flask and they wound down the windows to sip it, the sea breeze in their hair.

In the back of the van Rishi sipped his chai but did not want to leave the graceful unicorn. She seemed to have accepted his friendship and was happy for him to sit near her at least.

They were the only passengers, along with a few fishermen. Rishi was sure the unicorn hunters would be tracking them, but at least they were safe for now.

The sea swirled full of stars and the two mums laughed as the salt kissed their cheeks. Anisha's phone pinged and she popped her head round the back of the van to read it to Rishi. But her mouth fell open in dismay.

May Day! May Day!

Dash is overboard! We couldn't stop him. He broke out of the ship's cabin, barged through the dining room, upsetting an awful lot of diners, and then leapt over the side of the boat. Mum got a bit stressed, but luckily Caleb knew where the lifeboats were, and we managed to haul one over the side and climb down – even Rufus. It was very dramatic!

Caleb says he was right. It is like the Titanic! Only with a much better ending.

We are now rowing after Dash. I don't know where exactly we are, but we can still hear that music – it's kind of familiar?

I'll send coordinates when we reach land. Please, you must come and rescue us otherwise we'll be lost at sea forever...

Kx

"How will we find them?" gasped Anisha.

At that moment, Lumi stood up, her horn flashing like ice in moonlight, her mane and tail swishing superbly.

"Do you hear that?" asked Esme, pressing her hand to her heart, as she felt the same sharp tug as the unicorn.

Anisha shook her head, but Rishi focused inwards, and there, like a silver melody, was a thread of music, coiling itself around his heart.

"We must follow the music," Esme whispered, looking worried. "It is the only way to find Dash and the others, but we need to be careful. We could be sailing straight into a trap."

"Who on earth do you think is playing this music out in the middle of the sea?" asked Anisha, looking mightily confused.

Esme glanced at the inscription inside the viola. "My guess is Madame de Souza," she said. And with that she climbed out of the van, drew her dressing gown around her and went to speak to the captain.

CHAPTER ELEVEN
THE SONG OF THE SEA

Elodie, Marnie-Mae, Max and Stormy were having the most marvellous time aboard Silke's boat: *The Midnight Pearl*. Around them the night was deep and starry, the sea glittering with watery enchantments. Moonlight reflected beautifully upon the waves. Lanterns strung around the edge of the boat twinkled like secrets, and the air tasted of salt and myths.

Marnie-Mae had checked her phone for updates, but there was no signal, so all they could do was hope that all was well.

The swell of the sea rocked the little boat to and fro like a seashell, but Silke was a tremendous sailor. She had spent the first part of the journey teaching Max and the girls all her captain's orders. And so together they navigated their way across the icy waters. Even Stormy joined in by holding the sail taut between her teeth.

"Do you still play the harp?" asked Elodie, gazing at the case which rested at one end of the boat.

Silke nodded. "All the time. Not professionally, of course. My days with the orchestra are over, so now I mostly teach. But I love to play at pubs and festivals – even at sea."

"Will you play for us now?" Marnie begged, wide-eyed with wonder.

Silke obliged, letting Max steer *The Midnight Pearl* as she opened the case, settled herself near the hull, ran her fingers gently over glistening gold strings and began to play and sing. It was the most joyful melody any of them had ever heard. A song of sea-mist and tidal tales with a quick merry little tune.

In no time at all, Elle and Marnie were dancing and laughing along to words they didn't know as Stormy stamped and clattered around them. It was almost as much fun as skating!

It was only when it began to rain that Silke packed the beautiful harp away, and the girls and the little unicorn ducked inside the boat's cosy cabin to go to bed.

Marnie-Mae was far too alert to sleep and braided Stormy's mane instead. Elodie snuggled down and let her eyes close, and the memory of the music lulled her to sleep. She slipped straight back into the same frozen dream she'd had before.

She was floating on an iceberg over the wild green sea. In the distance was the bone-white lighthouse emitting a single luminous beam. Then Elodie heard music: a song of waves and sea. It felt so familiar to her, that melody woven from silver. She saw Stormy dive deep beneath the surface, her scales glimmering and glowing like moonlight. A shadow moved in the top of the lighthouse, and Elodie felt her blood turn cold. Someone was studying Stormy. Then a figure draped in black emerged from the door and cast a net into the sea.

"No!" Elodie cried in alarm. The net crackled and hissed, shining the pale blue of lightning. The only thing that could capture a unicorn.

And in the dream, her heart broke for Stormy.

"Stop!" she tried to yell.

But the mysterious figure pulled a shining viola

from within its cloak and began to play the same silvery song, drawing Stormy up to the surface and straight into the open net.

A dog barked. The net fizzed and spat.

Elodie blinked her eyes awake in alarm.

"What's wrong, Elle?" asked Marnie, taking Elodie's hand.

"We've got to save Stormy!" she cried, glancing around for the little unicorn.

They found Stormy outside near the hull of the boat, leaning as far out to sea as she could, her horn pointing like a mythical figurehead.

"Don't let her go overboard," urged Elodie as she and Marnie flanked the little unicorn. They both laid a gentle hand upon her winter-white coat as the rain lashed down fiercely in their faces. The moment Elodie touched Stormy, she heard it. Or felt it, echoing through Stormy's heart: the musical call of the song of the sea. It seemed to tighten around Elodie's soul, as if she too couldn't escape its pull. She let go of Stormy and stepped back with a gasp.

"What's the matter, Elle?" asked Max.

Marnie wrapped her arms around the tense little unicorn, and Silke leaned down from the boat's sail to listen as Elodie recounted her dream.

"The music in the dream is wrong," she said, shaking her curls out in frustration as lightning zapped and zinged through them. "The song is enchanting Stormy, drawing her in so that whoever is in the lighthouse can capture her and..." She broke off, too upset to continue.

"Tell me about the figure draped in black," said Silke curiously.

"A woman, I think, very glamorous, and somehow I knew she was terribly sad. She had a gleaming viola. She might have a dog – I'm not sure. I definitely heard a dog barking in my dream, it sounded very sad too. And whoever the woman is, she's incredibly powerful."

Silke considered this a moment, her face drawn and serious. "She sounds a lot like a woman I used to know at the orchestra. Lola de Souza. We knew her as Madame de Souza. She could play any instrument that had strings without reading a single musical note. You see, Lola was blind and played everything by ear. She was an exquisite musician, and she had a wonderful guide dog called Morgana. They were inseparable. They went everywhere together. With

Morgana at her side, Madame de Souza played concerts all over the world and lived a wonderful life."

"What happened to her?" asked Max.

"She left her position at the orchestra when Morgana became sick. She wanted to seek out a special vet who lived on a remote island, and I haven't heard from her since. I remember her two favourite students were distraught when she left. They were willing to do anything to help her cure Morgana."

"Who were they?" asked Marnie suddenly.

"Oh gosh, it was a little while ago. Yake? I think one of them was called Yake. Yake and … Yosh! That was it, Yake and Yosh," answered Silke. "They were such good musicians, such talented young men. Until Lola left and they became desperate."

"And they love classical music?" asked Elodie, glancing at Marnie.

"Of course!" replied Silke brightly.

"Does one have blonde hair, and the other a ginger beard?" Marnie urged, unable to take the suspense.

"Yes … but how did you know?" asked Silke.

"They're the unicorn kidnappers! The men in the van!" Marnie yelped, alarming Stormy but managing not to let go of her.

"One of them must also be a Unicorn Seeker," Elodie went on, "as they managed to catch Stormy's mum. Perhaps they've been trying to capture Stormy to bring her to Madame de Souza. So that poor Morgana can get better, and Madame de Souza could return to the orchestra with her beloved guide dog."

"But why Stormy?" said Max, a deep frown forming.

"There's nothing more powerful than a baby unicorn's horn," breathed Elodie, feeling quite sick with worry.

At that moment, the sea calmed, the weather stilled and a soft swirl of snowflakes danced from the sky. Then, sleek as silk, the tune of a viola filled the air, drawing the boat windlessly towards the moon.

"What's happening?" asked Max, stepping nearer to the two girls.

"I think we are reaching the lighthouse my sister spoke of in her letter," Silke murmured as they floated nearer.

"We have to turn the boat around! Sail away! Stormy's in danger..." Elodie pleaded.

"I'm afraid we cannot," said Silke softly. "The boat is sailing of its own accord."

The sea around them was a dark emerald dotted with small icebergs, and the only sound was the music of the viola. Elodie gasped as she watched her dream unfurling before her, as if the boat had sailed into her memories. There in the distance, casting a long shadow, was a lighthouse white as bone, a single ghostly beam illuminating the water. Stormy lunged forwards, and everyone lurched into action.

"Help me! Hold her, Elle!" called Marnie-Mae as the little unicorn tried to bolt. Elodie threw her arms around Stormy and closed her eyes, sending her thoughts straight to Stormy's heart.

STAY.

The pull of the sea and the silvery song were too great. Stormy's body was supple, strong, and so cold to touch. For a moment she didn't feel like a unicorn at all. And all at once, she slipped through Elodie and Marnie's embrace and jumped over the side of *The Midnight Pearl* and plunged into the deep green sea. Max yelled, Silke cursed, Marnie-Mae screamed and Elodie felt her eyes filling with tears as she clung to the side of the boat in despair.

As they stared down into the starry sea, a wondrous sight met them. Stormy's horn was aglow like a lantern, lighting up the world beneath the waves. All around her the water shimmered and sparkled, and for a moment it seemed as if the little horse was covered in scales that glimmered and glowed like moonlight.

"She's a mer-horse," whispered Marnie, "or a mermecorn?"

"A merry-corn," Silke concluded.

The air around them grew colder, the music ceased and the door to the bone-white lighthouse flew open. Everyone drew back in alarm apart from Elodie, who remembered this moment from her dream and stepped forward, determined to be ready this time.

A figure swept out of the lighthouse. Her skin was the black of magical midnights. Her coiled hair was woven regally into braids. Her black velvet robe flowed all the way to her ankles, and she carried herself like a queen. And beside her, leaning lovingly against the woman's legs, was a night-dark dog, who

padded gently on her fragile paws. And everyone saw that they were completely a team, like two souls who shared the same heart.

Poise and power seemed to radiate from the woman, and for a moment, Elodie felt afraid.

"Who is she?" asked Marnie.

"Lola de Souza," Silke confirmed. And her beloved guide dog Morgana.

As everyone on the boat peered at the phenomenal figure and her dog, they realized their bond was as deep as magic. As if together they could conquer the world.

"No wonder she wants to save her dog," whispered Marnie, "it's like they're family."

Elodie nodded, feeling a ripple of sadness for the beautiful black dog who clearly adored her owner.

Lola de Souza drew a magnificent viola from within the folds of her robe and began to play with the grace of someone conducting the clouds. This was the tune that had echoed across South London from the windows of the grey van. The tune that had whispered through Elodie's dreams. The tune which could draw a boat across a windless sea. A song so soft and true it could steal the stars from the Nordic night, or beg the sky to part with the moon, or call a unicorn up from the deep.

As Stormy crested the surface, Morgana gave a soft whine and Madame de Souza put down her viola and reached for a fearsome blue net from within the lighthouse. It flickered and flared with electricity. She placed it carefully beside Morgana for her to guard as she resumed her playing.

"No," said Elodie defiantly as she let her curls rise around her into a crackling halo, ready to step in and defuse the net. She focused her mind to try and find Stormy, who had disappeared back under the water. But at that moment another sound reached her ears: the soft lapping of something disturbing the waves.

They all turned to see a lifeboat bobbing across the still waters, also drawn in by the song. And in the lifeboat was Kit, looking keen-hearted and ready for adventure; Caleb, who was shivering and looking slightly seasick; Sophia, who seemed quite amazed by everything she saw; and Rufus, who was quietly whimpering on Caleb's lap.

Where's Dash? Elodie wondered hotly, but she

didn't dare take her focus off the net.

Kit stood up and waved wildly as soon as he saw them. Marnie ran to the edge of the boat and tried to yell to him. "That's Madame de Souza. She's trying to catch Stormy!"

At that moment Morgana began leading Madame de Souza carefully to the edge of the iceberg as Madame de Souza kept beautifully playing, nudging the lightning net with her foot. "That's Morgana, her guide dog," Marnie tried to explain. "Morgana is not well. Madame de Souza is trying to save her life."

Kit and Caleb both focused on the midnight-black dog. Her eyes were kind and wise as the stars, seeing everything her owner did not, and ensuring with the utmost love that Madame de Souza did not slip, or misstep on the ice. Morgana – looked magnificent – but she moved so slowly, as if each step hurt her bones.

Elodie watched the way Morgana and Lola de Souza were completely in sync, as if their minds were linked. And it reminded her of the deep bond she'd shared with Astra and now with Stormy. Her eyes flashed to Caleb and Rufus, huddled together in the boat. Suddenly Elodie understood.

"Madame de Souza needs Stormy's horn to save Morgana's life," she breathed as the truth of it hit her. "Perhaps she doesn't know it will kill Stormy. We need to be nearer. I have to speak to her," she cried, and Silke and Max tried to catch what little wind there was, steering *The Midnight Pearl* as close to the bone-white lighthouse as they could.

The moment they were close enough, Elodie and Marnie-Mae scrambled over the edge of the deck and landed on ice. It was slippery and cool through their slippers, but the girls were excellent skaters, and it was easy for them to glide effortlessly towards Madame de Souza.

Hearing them approach, she paused her playing and turned to face them. Morgana gave a soft growl from her side. "I wouldn't come any closer if I were you," said Madame de Souza in a formal tone, "not unless you wish to end up snared by the net as well."

"No, we definitely don't," said Elodie calmly, giving Marnie-Mae the tiniest wink.

"We sure don't," Marnie agreed. "We'd never get out."

"What is it you want?" asked Madame de Souza,

her voice as deep and velvety as her splendid robe.

"To ask you to spare the little unicorn," said Elodie earnestly. "We know why you want her horn. It's the only thing that can cure your beloved guide dog. But if you take Stormy's horn, you'll take her life."

"Like … isn't there an amazing vet we can all go to? We could help you crowdfund the expenses," Marnie added, but Madame de Souza gave a sad shake of her head.

"Do you think I haven't tried?" she replied, her voice low and pained. "I'm so very sorry about the little unicorn. I truly wish there was another way. But Morgana has such little time left, I can't wait any longer. She is not just my sight, but my heart and soul," Madame de Souza explained regretfully.

And with that she turned away from them and resumed her song with renewed energy.

Stormy came shooting up from the water, as if she were running through the waves. The lightning net crackled at Lola de Souza's feet. Marnie-Mae took a breath and dived towards it, skidding across the ice. Years of ballet and karate made her brave and graceful all at once. She felt the heat and rage of the net and tried to kick it far into the sea, away from the approaching Stormy, but Morgana gently nudged Marnie out of the way, and she tripped, almost slipping into the cold water.

Sensing the commotion, Madame de Souza tucked the viola and bow back into the deep pockets of her robe and carefully raised the net into the air.

Elodie moved into position, focusing her energy on Stormy, trying to send her thoughts to her.

The net was tossed high, seeming to float and dazzle before slowly descending on to the sea's surface.

Elodie sprang forward. There was a splitting of waves and a swooshing of air and then a unicorn of bright magnificence launched out of the water, his horn dagger-sharp, his eyes wild sapphires.

"DASH!"

Everyone gasped. Elodie skidded to a halt as Dash sped into the net, his hooves pushing little bright-eyed Stormy out of the way. The baby unicorn spun in the water, then dived deep. The strands of blue lightning fizzed and spat, closing around Dash, sealing him in. Morgana howled and Madame de

Souza swore crossly as she wrestled the net out of the sea, realizing from the sheer weight that she had not captured the baby, but something far larger.

Elodie fell to her knees in shock, teetering on the edge of the iceberg. Marnie-Mae slid over to her. "At least it's not Stormy," she breathed as they stared nervously at the wildly thrashing Dash.

"But we still need to free him, or it won't be long before Stormy comes to find him," Elodie whispered back, closing her eyes, trying to reach him with her mind.

Unicorns respond to love, she thought, trying desperately to make a connection. She could sense his bright white anger like a flame at the edge of her mind.

But a regal figure and a black dog stepped between her and Dash. The music of the viola filled the air once more, breaking Elodie's connection and sending Dash to sleep. As the wondrous unicorn sank to the ice, closing his eyes and laying his head down, Elodie trembled. If she couldn't reach Dash, how would she ever free him?

A little shout came across the sea and the lifeboat

bobbed closer. Kit, Caleb and Rufus pulled Elodie and Marnie into the lifeboat, forming a protective ring around Elodie as her hair crackled and fizzed.

"Don't forget your destiny," said Kit kindly, taking Elodie's hand.

"Or your heritage," Caleb added in a quiet voice. "You come from a long line of Unicorn Seekers."

Sophia nodded her encouragement, not quite sure how to help.

Even though Elodie's heart was breaking for Dash and little Stormy deep beneath the sea, she thought suddenly of her great-grandmother Elyse de Lyon: a woman for whom a unicorn had given its life for long ago. And then she remembered the power gifted to whoever a unicorn had saved. How it could transcend generations.

Now is the time to use that power, she thought, feeling the bright burn of hope sweep over her.

"If Dash can visit me in dreams, maybe I can visit him too…" she murmured. "I just need to be able wake him."

CHAPTER TWELVE
A SEEKER'S WISH

"That's a great idea, Elle," cried Kit, instantly making a note of it in his notebook. "But does that mean you need to go to sleep?"

"I think I just need to meditate or something."

"Let me help," Sophia said, beaming.

Elodie sat cross-legged in the bobbing boat with all her friends gathered around her as Sophia instructed. She let every thought fade until her mind was filled with peace. Far beneath the iceberg Elodie sensed the magic and motion of Stormy, prancing and spinning joyfully through the waves. She smiled, knowing that Stormy was exactly where she belonged.

Gently she closed her mind to her, leaving the little merry-corn to explore the wild ways of the sea. They did not have long before the pull of the song brought Stormy swimming back to the surface. Now she felt the feral energy of Dash and she stepped towards it, slipping soundlessly into his dream. At first there was only darkness, and the bewitching tune of the viola. Then, all the unicorn's imaginings came rushing to her: images of Stormy when she was very young, Stormy's astonishing mother racing through the waves, the feeling of cantering through the midnight streets of South London.

In the dream Elodie stood outside her bright blue front door and raised her unicorn whistle to her lips, blowing into the pink shell as Dash came charging past. But the whistle made no sound. Elodie needed another way to wake him. She followed him, skating through the sleepy streets, calling and calling his name. And then she sensed something else. A light that kept flickering and flashing at the edge of her consciousness, like the gleam of a distant star. In Dash's dream, Elodie skated towards it, her heart quickening as she heard the pound of hooves and hot crackle of lightning.

She sat forward on the boat, her hazelnut eyes blinking open. "I can't wake Dash," she gasped, "but I know who can." She pointed out over the vast waves, between the icebergs, to a freight ship that was massively off course. The hunters' van was parked upon its deck, surrounded by a very confused captain and several befuddled fishermen. The boat was being drawn across the water by the song of the sea. Peering wildly out of the van's windows were Maman and Anisha.

"Where's Rishi?" asked Kit.

"Probably in the back with Lumi," answered Caleb.

"Who's Lumi?" Marnie frowned. She and Elodie were quite astounded to see the van on a boat in the middle of the Nordic Sea.

"Lumi is Stormy's mum," Caleb explained.

"I need to get on to that boat before Lumi falls under the music's spell. She can help me wake Dash," Elodie cried, and they all grabbed paddles – even Caleb was highly fed up with getting splashed, but he was very serious about saving unicorns – and fought against the tug of the song to reach the freight ship. It was like trying to paddle through fog, the sea barely stirring, the boat hardly moving.

Then, all at once, Stormy's horn crested the waves, her legs kicking hard, her nose nudging the lifeboat forward.

"She's amazing!" Marnie said, laughing triumphantly.

"How did she know to help us?" Sophia marvelled.

"I asked her to," said Caleb simply, making everyone smile.

"Keep her safe while I free Lumi!" Elodie beamed.

Caleb nodded as Stormy leapt into the lifeboat, soaking them all. Only this time Caleb didn't mind – Stormy's safety was too important.

"As long as we can keep her in the boat, we can buy ourselves some time," said Kit, quickly finding a gluten-free blueberry muffin to share with her.

Elodie and Marnie climbed the rusted red ladder on the side of the freight ship. The moment they were on deck, Elodie felt the power of the mother unicorn radiating from the back of the van.

Let me help you, she said with her mind, opening the van's doors.

The unicorn gazed at her with a deep searching hope, her eyes as fierce as midwinter stars. Elodie held out her hands, feeling the scorch of the net. She smiled at Rishi, who was crouched behind Lumi, trying to calm her. Lumi's horn glowed.

"Be careful," whispered Maman, coming to stand with Anisha and Marnie-Mae.

Rishi lingered in the shadows at the back of the van, nodding a swift hello to Elodie. Elodie took a deep breath. She shook out her curls, and hurled herself into the fibres of the net. Her hair flew up around her and her heart filled with love for the unicorn and her family.

The net trembled and shook as every strand of lightning found a tendril of Elodie's hair. Elodie scrambled out of the van, the net and the beautiful unicorn coming with her. She twirled upon the deck, her hair alight like fireworks. Thunder struck the clouds as rain poured sleekly from the sky. Lumi reared up fiercely and the net broke, carried away like a ball of magic back into the night. Elodie shook out her curls. Lightning raged from the ends of them, striking the door of the van so it fell from its hinges. And then the storm was over.

Elodie felt Maman embrace her, stroking her crackling curls away from her face. "My girl of stars and storms," Maman whispered, kissing Elodie's cheek.

Marnie took Elodie's hand. And Rishi came rushing out of the van gasping. "That was awesome," he whispered, completely in awe.

Anisha dropped her chai. When Elodie defused the lighting net, Anisha had seen as clear as day that Lumi was a unicorn. She stood blinking in amazement.

"We have to save Dash," said Elodie, ignoring the small crowd of fishermen.

Lumi moved towards Elodie. She was pale as a cloud and graceful as starlight. Elodie dipped her head in greeting, then tenderly stroked Lumi's long nose, gently nuzzling until she felt the bright flare of the unicorn's thoughts.

We have to wake Dash up.

Lumi raised her head in understanding.

At the helm of the rusty red freight ship, Elodie and Lumi faced the lighthouse where a figure draped in velvet was still playing her spellbinding viola and where a unicorn slept beneath a crackling blue net. Together they slipped into Dash's dream.

This time in Dash's dream, when Dash raced through the lovely leafy park, Lumi was waiting for him by the lake. She reared up in warning, and on the iceberg Dash's sapphire-blue eyes flashed open. But all he could do was raise his head, the musical melody lulling him into a sleepless still.

"Maybe we can stop the music," said Maman, seizing the viola from the front of the grey van and tossing it over to her husband. Max caught the viola and began to play a folk song. He wasn't exactly an amazing musician, but he could certainly hold a tune.

Silke seized her golden harp and joined in. Kit and Sophia started clapping along, while Caleb covered his ears to block the whole thing out. Rufus howled, Stormy stamped and Elodie felt as if she were at a folk festival on the sea.

Morgana looked out sadly towards them and Elodie felt a pang of sympathy. The dog had such wise eyes, as if she knew they were trying to break the spell and she understood the cost. Lola's viola faltered for a moment but the tune did not cease. An outraged cry cut through the music as a speedboat came speeding furiously over the waves.

"It's the men from the van!" said Maman in alarm.

"Yake and Yosh," Silke muttered.

The men soared swiftly to the lighthouse, where the blonde man – Yake – leapt out and informed Lola de Souza of everything he knew.

The man with the ginger beard – Yosh – then zoomed across the water to *The Midnight Pearl*, climbed aboard, and began to wrestle with Max for his viola. Silke struck him with her bow but he clung on to the viola.

Things were getting out of control and Elodie was still struggling to summon Dash. She raised her unicorn whistle to her lips and let the high-pitched sound ring out. Dash stood up. It was all Elodie needed. She dived over the side of the boat. The cold green sea soothed her crackling hair as she swam to the iceberg. Dash whinnied in gratitude and Elodie launched herself into the net. Bolts of lightning fired in all directions. Morgana howled, Rufus growled, Dash reared up, a creature of myth and marvels, and the net broke, blue tendrils of lightning finding Elodie's curls, as the sky was split by thunder until the clouds swooped in and swept away the storm.

A silence fell across the deep green sea. Dash stood proud and magnificent at Elodie's side. Everyone on the freight ship, *The Midnight Pearl* and the lifeboat had their hands clasped over their mouths. Elodie felt a swift tug at her heart and she gasped as Lumi, Stormy and Dash all locked eyes, their horns glowing brighter than the stars reflected on the sea.

All three unicorns leapt through the air, crossing

each other's paths in an arc of love and freedom before they plunged into the sea and disappeared below, diving to depths unknown.

Lola de Souza gave a piercing scream, her viola clattering on to the ice as Yake told her what had happened.

Elodie knelt beside Morgana, trying to ignore the terrible ache in her heart, the pain of the unicorns departing. Out of the corner of her eye she could see Marnie-Mae quietly crying, Rishi looking amazed, Maman wilting with relief, Kit peering into the water, seeing if he could follow the glimmer of the unicorns below, and Caleb sadly watching Morgana, his arms around Rufus. Sensing the terrible sorrow that Madame de Souza was dealing with.

"Oh, my beautiful girl, I'm so sorry I've failed you. But we won't ever give up," Madame de Souza wept as Morgana sadly licked her face.

Elodie beckoned gently to Caleb and as the lifeboat bobbed closer, he stepped out and knelt beside her. Without saying a word, Elodie took the little silver tub from her pocket and opened the lid. First came the aroma of rain on a midsummer's eve,

then the saltiness of the sea, followed by frost and a pinch of moonlight. Caleb put a dab upon his fingers and with great care smoothed it over Morgana's heart. Elodie closed her eyes and made a wish, using her seeker's power, the talent gifted from her great-grandmother. At once everything calmed and there was only the watery sound of the waves. Morgana stood up and shook out her silky coat, giving Caleb a surprise lick on the cheek.

"What is that curious scent?" asked Madame de Souza as Morgana shook out her fabulous fur and nudged her to her feet.

"Nothing much." Elodie smiled. "But let's just say Morgana should be OK for a little while longer. Well ... for the rest of your life I should think."

Lola de Souza put her hands over her mouth in amazement. She was quite overcome with emotion. "Thank you. Thank you," she whispered, reaching out to grasp Elodie and Caleb's hands.

"You are welcome," said Elodie kindly, "but you must swear that you will never ever enchant another unicorn again, with music or a lighting net or through any other magic you might know."

"I swear upon Morgana's life," she promised, as the beautiful dog slunk happily around her legs, barking in swift delight.

And as the clouds cleared and the autumn moon lit the sea's surface, deep and shimmering, they all boarded boats to set sail for Reykjavik's harbour. Kit, Caleb, Sophia, Rufus and Rishi joined the crew of *The Midnight Pearl*. Meanwhile, Anisha and Esme accompanied Yake, Yosh and Madame de Souza aboard the freight ship where they began their lecture on being more responsible for the safety of unicorns. Maman even made them all sign a special contract to say they would only use their gifts and knowledge to protect unicorns from now on. Morgana signed a paw print on behalf of Madame de Souza. Yake and Yosh hung their heads, quietly explaining that they had stumbled across the lightning nets at an old market in Sweden. They had been so distraught when Madame de Souza had departed from the orchestra, they wanted to do anything they could to help.

"How did you know where to search for them?" asked Maman sternly.

"There is a Braille copy of Ava Bjornson's diary in the local library," Lola de Souza explained. "Ava was the sister of the arctic explorer Byron Bjornson, and her research around unicorns is quite spectacular. Most people think her notes are a work of fiction. But once I had the net, I knew it was real."

"Where's the Braille diary now?"

"Safe in the library, categorized under 'myths and legends'... I doubt many folk will think it's real," she went on. "And we have no need to ever harm unicorns." Lola smiled. "Now my beloved Morgana is well, I can return to my work, my students and my life." She turned her face in Elodie's direction. "I can't thank you enough. We will instead do everything we can to help protect these wonderful creatures."

As they sailed the path of the moon, Max began singing a folk song and Silke strummed her golden harp. Elodie and all of her friends stood together gazing out to sea. Just as the bone-white lighthouse vanished from view, Elodie thought she saw a boat in the distance with a woman onboard gladly waving.

She turned to Silke, who nodded at her and winked. "The sea is full of many marvels. Some too strange for us to ever understand," said the harpist warmly.

"Makes sense," said Caleb. "We've only explored eight per cent of the world's oceans. No one really knows what goes on in the deep dark sea."

Elodie thought back to her dream of mermaids and merrows coming to welcome Stormy and she laughed softly.

"Well, we certainly know that there's a herd of Winter's Dawn living down there," said Kit brightly.

"And maybe lots of other unicorns and mythical sea creatures too – who knows! We could start a whole new blog," added Marnie.

"Or you could tell us when you visit Stormy's dreams," said Rishi to Elodie.

Harp music filled the air again. Madame de Souza, Yake and Yosh joined Silke's song on their violas. They played tunes that were folky and fun and filled with deep-sea joy. The two dogs howled along to the melody and everyone started dancing.

Even though Elodie's heart felt bruised from

saying goodbye to Stormy, she was elated knowing that any time she wished, she could focus her mind and slip into a unicorn's dream. And that felt like the most magical thing in all the world.

CHAPTER THIRTEEN
SIX MINUTES TO SUNRISE

At six minutes to sunrise in the vast city of London, where the sky can turn from brightest blue to golden grey in the blink of an eye, Elodie Lightfoot gazed out across the lovely leafy park below her flat, her heart stirring with wonder and joy at all that had unfolded.

October rain fell gently against the windows, colouring the day sea-mist grey. The sound of Max and Esme laughing in the kitchen echoed down the hall, along with the scent of *Parfum de Rose* and the blueberry sweetness of muffin mix. Elodie beamed and sat up, smoothing her mass of spiralling ringlets into a bun. She gasped as the little darts of lightning shocked her fingers.

"Six minutes till we leave, Elle. You almost

ready?" Max called.

Six minutes later, the three of them set off together. "It's perfect weather for croissants," Max said cheerfully, and Elodie couldn't help smiling despite the tender ache in her heart. A bruise the shape of a baby unicorn.

Marnie came flying over the tarmac on her roller skates, sweeping Elodie into a hug. Elodie pulled on her rainbow-laced roller skates and flew after Marnie towards their friends – the best Unicorn Seekers in all of South London. She high-fived Kit and Caleb and stroked Rufus' ears as they pored over Kit's notebook. They would meet Rishi later after school and go over it with him too.

It was all there. Everything they'd learned about Stormy, Dash and Lumi. All their adventures on the Nordic Sea. There was even a sketch of the mysterious lighthouse and of Silke's harp.

"So we know loads about Winter's Dawns," Marnie chattered, "but I wonder which glory we'll discover next."

"I'm not sure." Elodie sighed as they glided towards the dinosaur statues.

She loved this time of morning, when every dream for the day felt possible. The boating lake was all the colours of autumn, dew sparkled upon purple asters and in the soft early light if she looked at the much-loved statues, Elodie could almost imagine they were real. The wind stirred the golden-brown leaves and Elodie stumbled and glanced behind her. For a moment she was sure she'd seen something the same warm gold as the leaves. Perhaps a deer or even a large sandy dog. But there was nothing. Only the swaying branches, the lake and the misty London skies.

She glanced at Caleb, but he was busy with Rufus so she skated on. She didn't notice him drop a chunk of blueberry muffin on to the leaf-layered ground. Nor did she hear the little thankful whinny from a horse the colour of sand. It had pale grey eyes and hooves the pink of seashells. And as it emerged from beneath the trees, Caleb could just make out its dagger sharp horn and sea-foam mane.

"A Surf Dancer," he murmured in quiet awe. He turned and smiled to himself, before gliding dreamily on.

Oak Grove community garden

South of the Misty River
London, late autumn

What to do if you find a unicorn behind the recycling bins!

Dear Reader,

Hello! I'm Rishi, a totally regular boy from South London. Until very recently I thought unicorns were a myth, or a legend, or at the very least extinct. But it turns out I was totally wrong!

You see, one evening this huge, mysterious horse just showed up randomly in our community garden. I thought he was pretty cool and he seemed friendly, so when it started to rain, I stayed with him and then the most incredible thing happened. I could hardly believe it ... the horse became wildly excited and started charging around the garden. When lightning struck, he transformed before my very eyes into a unicorn. It was epic, like something from a dream. I sensed him communicating, like he was sending me his thoughts, and I found out his name was Dash.

Pretty soon it became clear that Dash was in some kind of danger and he couldn't keep on hiding out behind the recycling bins. I knew I had to try and keep him safe - so this is what I did.

I read this brilliant blog and wrote to the Unicorn Seekers (I still wasn't certain anyone would really believe me).

Then I went to meet the Unicorn Seekers at lunchtime, as two of them go to my school. Luckily, they were really nice and super encouraging. They believed me straightaway. They knew so much about unicorn lore and the history (like all the different glories and where they're from, what their habitats are and which foods they prefer).

We all went on an astonishing adventure to Iceland to rescue Dash's family and reunite them. It was wild, a little scary, but so magical to witness.

I think it's the best thing that's ever happened to me. The amazing thing is, it could happen to you too!

I found out there are so many Unicorn Seekers all over the world who haven't yet discovered their gifts. Maybe you dream of unicorns? Perhaps you've spotted a unicorn's shadow when everyone else saw a horse? Or maybe you've even seen a real-life unicorn at the bottom of your garden like I did.

So keep seeking with an open heart, and if you ever find a unicorn that needs help, please get in touch through this blog. Marnie-Mae checks it every weekday morning in the computer room and Elodie or Kit check it at weekends. If you're in London, we will try to meet you IRL at a skate park. If you're from anywhere else in the world we can set up a group chat. We might even send you a sequin unicorn badge!

Thanks so much for reading! I've got to go now. Kit and Caleb are here to teach me how to roller-skate.

Wish me luck.

And never give up on believing in unicorns.

Rishi

ABOUT THE AUTHOR

Cerrie Burnell is an author, actor and ambassador best known for her work on CBeebies, a role which has earned her critical recognition and a devoted fan base. During her time on CBeebies, she has broken down barriers, challenged stereotypes and overcome discrimination to become one of the most visible disabled presenters on kids' TV.

Cerrie is the author of twelve children's books, including *Snowflakes*, which she adapted for the stage with the Oxford Playhouse in 2016, and the *Harper* series, which includes a book that was a World Book Day title in 2016. She has also created a one woman show, *The Magical Playroom*, which premiered at the Edinburgh Fringe in 2013.

Since leaving CBeebies, Cerrie has appeared in the BBC continuing drama *Doctors* and made the eye-opening documentary *Silenced* for the BBC. Her newest book *I Am Not A Label* published in 2020 and was one of Amazon US's "Twenty best children's nonfiction books" of 2020 and was the overall children's choice winner of the SLA 2021 Information Book Award.

Cerrie is currently the BBC's ambassador for disability.

Photo by Lynda Kelly